HERMETIC MEDITATION

Martin Faulks

Copyright © 2021 by Martin Faulks
All rights reserved. This book or any portion thereof may not be reproduced or used in any manner whatsoever without the express written permission of the publisher except for the use of brief quotations in a book review or scholarly journal.

Cover and interior design by Tanya Robinson
Edited by Kendall Moore
Published by Falcon Books Publishing Ltd
First Printing: 2021

FALCON BOOKSPUBLISHING LTD
71-75 Sheldon Street Covent Garden.
London, WCH 9JQ
www.falconbookspublishing.com
Copyright © 2021 Martin Faulks
All rights reserved.

ISBN -13: 978-1-8384598-0-2

Ordering Information:
Hardback copies are available on the Falcon Books Publishing website:

www.falconbookspublishing.com

This book is dedicated to the students of the Seshen School of Hermetic Meditation.

Only when our knowledge of inner technologies and abilities matches our outer progress will we reach our full potential.

- Martin Faulks

Titles by the Author

Butterfly Tai Chi (Gateways to Health Series), Watkins Publishing (2009).

Gateways to Health: Secrets Of Rejuvenation, Watkins Publishing (2009).

Becoming the Lotus (2009).

The Masonic Detective, Lulu.com, Talbort J (2012).

The Path of the Ninja-An Englishman's quest to master the secrets of Japan's invisible assassins Ian Allan Publishing (2015).

The Emerald Tablet-A Commentary on The True Path of an Adept (2015).

Shugendo-The Way of the Mountain Monks (In conjunction with Shokai Koshikidake) Faulks Books (2015).

Enlightened Living, Falcon Books Publishing (2017).

Adepthood, Success on All Levels, Falcon Books Publishing (2018).

Future Titles

The Soul Mirrors, Falcon Books Publishing.

The Secret Teaching of the Cosmic Maiden, Falcon Books Publishing.

TABLE OF CONTENTS

TABLE OF CONTENTS v
INTRODUCTION vii
SECTION 1 FOUNDATIONS OF HERMETIC TRAINING 1
CHAPTER 1 WHAT IS HERMETICISM ?: 3
Who was Hermes Trismegistus? 3
The Heart of Hermetics 4
CHAPTER 2: WHAT IS MEDITATION AND HOW DOES IT WORK? 5
The History of Meditation 7
CHAPTER 3: THE TRUE PURPOSE OF MEDITATION 9
Righteous Action 11
CHAPTER 4: BENEFITS OF MEDITATION 13
Ten Benefits of Any Authentic Meditation Practice 13
CHAPTER 5: HERMETIC MEDITATION – TUNING INTO THE GREAT GOOD 17
CHAPTER 6: HERMETIC PRINCIPLES FOR MEDITATION 21
The Method of Hermetic Meditation Revealed 21
Creating a Space for Meditation Practice 26
CHAPTER 7: CHOOSING A MEDITATION POSTURE 29
Progressive Meditation Postures for Beginners and More Advanced Practitioners 29
Four Main Progressive Meditation Postures 30
Lotus Posture 38
CHAPTER 8: HOW TO MEDITATE 43
A Detailed Method of Hermetic Meditation 43
Some Queries Addressed Regarding Experiences During Meditation Practice 46

CHAPTER 9: MEDITATION TOOLS..51

Meditation Tools: Why Do We Use Them?..51

CHAPTER 10: RITUAL DISCPLINES OF MEDITATION..55

CHAPTER 11: HOW TO STICK TO A MEDITATION ROUTINE.............................59

Methods to Establish a Meditation Routine..61

Learning from Distractions that Occur During Meditation Practice..............................63

SECTION 2: INVITING THE GREAT GOOD INTO DAILY LIFE 67

CHAPTER 12: FORMING A REGULAR AND BALANCED LIFESTYLE.................69

CHAPTER 13: THE EYE OF THE HORUS – BEING IN EVERY MOMENT............73

CHAPTER 14: HOW TO DEAL WITH PERSISTENT DISTURBANCES..................77

CHAPTER 15: BRINGING THE GOOD MIND INTO YOUR DAILY LIFE...............83

CHAPTER 16: REGULATING AND BALANCING THE MIND..................................87

CHAPTER 17: ADJUSTMENT OF THE MIND THROUGH THE ADJUSTMENT OF ONES SPEECH..91

CHAPTER 18: HOW TO TURN PROCRASTINATION AND INNER CONFLICT TO YOUR ADVANTAGE...97

CHAPTER 19: INNER ACLHEMY..103

Making Friends with Negative Emotions...103

CHAPTER 20: ASSOCIATE THE GOOD WITHIN YOURSELF..............................113

CHAPTER 21: RECOGNISING SPIRITUAL TRUTH..115

CHAPTER 22: FURTHER METHODS TO STILL THE OR FOCUS THE MIND.....119

CHAPTER 23: OTHER FORMS OF HERMETIC MEDITATION............................121

Hermetic Practice of Inner Silence..121

ABOUT THE AUTHOR...123

INTRODUCTION

I remember the moment I first glimpsed the true nature of meditation.

Watch the breath as if it is precious and expand your awareness to match mine.

Once in the mountains, I was sitting with a great master practising the art of meditation. We were surrounded by nature and encompassed by a sense of pure serenity. He sat in a state of pure awareness. Fully awake, yet at one with his surroundings. His breathing was gentle, long, and rhythmical – his body firm and unmoving. I felt a sense of raised awareness just being in the presence of someone practising with such ability.

As I sat there, listening to the sounds of the animals in the woodland and the roar of the waterfall, I found myself drifting off and becoming distracted for a few moments. It is said that you can judge somebody on the company they keep, and this great practitioner chose to spend his time with the elements of nature. Today the sun, wind, and occasional rainfalls had come to bear witness to the truth of his teachings.

Then something very special happened. A change came across my being and I found myself in a state of pure thought. The object of my meditation was the enlightened master before me. As I sat there in silent harmony, my breathing, posture, and inner gaze had matched my teacher. In that moment it felt like we were in harmony with all that was good in the world and that by practising with someone more adept in this art I had been led to an ideal state of mind. The way of thinking and improved perception stayed with me for hours after this experience.

In the days following this experience, things came more into focus. I realised that beyond all the various teachings or religious trappings, meditation was simply the practice of reaching the ideal healthy state of human consciousness. From that day onwards, I made sure to take note of the effect that my meditation practice had on my everyday consciousness. I was sure to make an effort to bring the lessons from meditation into my daily life.

As the years passed, I increasingly realised the extreme value of meditation. Meditation has many health benefits and stress-reducing properties which are well documented, but few people talk about its ability to save us. I am not talking about being saved from some devil or divine punishment, but from ourselves. By practising meditation and acquiring this ideal state of consciousness, we gain clarity of focus that protects us from confusion. It allows us to be more actively involved in our lives and to guide it in the direction we wish. The ability to live a healthy, happy life and to direct it to make the most of your time is a great gift worth sharing.

The aim of this book is to present a guide to meditation from a modern and practical Hermetic perspective. The meditation technique used in this volume involves a focus on oneness with pure goodness. This is a technique that, although very much focused on in Hermetic teachings, is also greatly valued in various forms of many traditions across the world in both the East and West.

May this book guide you as my teacher did me.

SECTION 1

FOUNDATIONS OF HERMETIC TRAINING

Meditation is the ultimate skill, the mastery of which leads to mastery of all other skills.

~ Martin Faulks

WHAT IS HERMETICISM?

CHAPTER 1

Many people have heard the term Hermetic in the sense of something being Hermetically sealed, or of the Greek messenger god Hermes with his winged sandals and headbands. Few people are aware that the term Hermetic relates to a body of beautiful writings said to be produced by a figure called Hermes Trismegistus.

The revered works of Hermes Trismegistus appeared as textbooks for a group of inspired and enlightened people living in Greek occupied Egypt around AD 0-200. From the writings we learn they were high minded individuals with views and intentions advanced for their time. They were probably vegetarian, saw the genders as equal, and united in the goal of helping all living creatures. The works of Hermes Trismegistus focus on the evolution of human consciousness and present a comprehensive and universal philosophy that covers almost every aspect of life and creation. Its main focus is upon the nature of the divine and identifying the true purpose of human existence on earth. These works were created at a time when many different traditions were coming together and contain a blend of influences from diverse religious and philosophical teachings.

Who was Hermes Trismegistus?

Many traditions are named after a founder, real or imaginary, and the Hermeticum is no exception. The texts that make up the Hermetic tradition are said to be written by an enlightened teacher called Hermes Trismegistus, but who was this mysterious author?

The texts themselves never explain who he was, and there are multiple theories put forwards as part of the tradition. The most common and convincing theory is that Hermes Trismegistus, or the Egyptian Hermes, as he was often called, is a composite god. He consists of a combination of the Greek Hermes, a figure of cunning, guile, and both a herald and messenger and Thoth, the Egyptian god of magic, mystery, and writing, a scribe of the gods and keeper of the secrets of the universe. Theories exist that Hermes Trismegistus was the grandson of the Greek god Hermes or a reincarnated spiritual teacher, who continuously reincarnates to teach and guide mankind throughout history.

In the early writings, Hermes was always taken to be a literal, historical figure. In later times, however, people have often interpreted him as a symbolic figure who represents the ideal enlightened state. Some people even believe him to be an actual spirit that works through different authors, like a divine muse teaching though their words and writings.

The Heart of Hermetics

If we go back to the Western spiritual traditions of the past and compare the practices and goals of those schools with present-day schools, one vital principle would stand out, which has largely been lost or looked over. In those days, the purpose of the practice was to increasingly tune into, harmonise with, and to become one with the original underlying principle of existence, the substance from which all things came. This substance was not considered inert. It was living, dynamic, and positive. To understand how this idea was conceived, we can use the example of 'the Force' from Star Wars films. In ancient times, the concept of a dark side of the Force did not exist. It was perceived that all disharmony and chaos was caused by the Force not being present, as darkness is caused by lack of light. Different schools had different names for this underlying, primordial energy. The names they used have helped us understand how they felt and the way they could connect with it. For some people, it was 'the boundless.' For others it was 'the hidden.' Some felt you could tune into this energy through nature, so for them it was 'the natural' or 'the real.' Some people felt that it was the original abstract principle, 'the pure truth,' 'the light that shines on through all lights,' so they were looking for the truth. Many people felt that it was 'sense of pure consciousness,' 'the mind that thought up all things.'

To the Hermeticist, it was all of these and they called it 'The Great Good.' Through their training, reading, and practices, they would become at one with The Great Good and transform from a mortal to a divine being. When in tune with the Great Good, a wonderful sense of contentment and inner peace is acquired. These hidden forces open up to you, and great powers become yours. Your intuition takes on a universal nature as you witness the ebb and flow of the consciousness behind all. Because of this, the Hermeticists should be a force for good. They are bringing harmony wherever there is discord, order when there is chaos, and manifesting goodness into the world, in every thought, word, and action.

We need to bring this principal back to our Western tradition, making it the central aspiration so that we can bring genuine practice and firm achievements to our path. Through these ideals we can help the world.

WHAT IS MEDITATION AND HOW DOES IT WORK?

CHAPTER 2

One aim of meditation is to develop a full dedication to a subject or undertaking. The practitioner's mind must become like a focused beam of light shining completely on the subject—clear, bright, and unceasing. The practitioner is required to make his entire being rest and be calm. Any tension during meditation shows that part of you is not dedicated to the subject of focus, or that your mind is not working in a fully integrated way. Consciousness must be brought into harmony and be completely free from distraction, inner conflict, confusion, or mixed intentions.

The practice of meditation is well known for its multitude of health benefits. Meditation can improve physical healing from illness. It can help regulate blood pressure, cure depression, ease anxiety, and help with other mental illnesses. However, it is important to remember that these health benefits are not the aim of meditation, but they are side effects reflecting the inner harmony and balance brought about by meditation. As the practitioner develops his ability to meditate, he learns to confront internal challenges and face the causes of disruption that either exists within himself or is created by external events in his life. Without facing these challenges, one's meditation cannot improve.

As one learns to overcome these difficulties during meditation practice, you bring your life and inner being into harmony. Negative emotions are transformed, pains from the past are learned from and released, illnesses are cured, confusion disappears, and unproductive behaviours stop. Each time we overcome an obstacle, it can no longer disturb us during meditation practice, and our focus vastly improves. Our mastery of life and health improve, along with our ability to meditate.

All forms of meditation require internal effort to self-regulate the mind. Some choose to sit. Some practitioners meditate in a more active way, such as walking. Some people use mala or prayer beads or other ritual objects to keep track of the time spent focusing on a specific subject and aiding in recentering our focus. These are all mental aids, but in truth, all forms of meditation have the same goal, to be fully focused and aware of the subject of meditation.

As you continue your journey into the art of meditation, you may discover specific stages in your development. These are characterised by certain states of consciousness or refined levels of focus, as well documented by ancient masters. This inner unfolding can be related specifically to the four elements, or states of matter.

Earth

The Indian yogis call the first stage of attainment *Dharana*, relating to the element of earth and concentration. In the West, we talk about contemplation. In this state, we learn to let our focus rest on one point by holding it with a firm, immovable focus. Our mind becomes as solid as a rock or as stable as a mountain. We are imperturbable and immovable, and we hold the subject in focus through a sustained concentration. Our sustained attention continues to hone our focus and crystallize on the object. To master this ability, we need to have overcome all major disturbances or traumas in our personality and have a developed a balanced, healthy lifestyle.

Water

The second stage of attainment is known as *Dhyana,* or meditation to the yogis, and relates to liquids and the element of water. In this state, our mind is still focused on the object of meditation, but as our skill has developed, we have gained the ability to make our thoughts naturally flow towards a subject. Our mind is like a river, constantly moving towards the object of meditation naturally. By staying aware and not forgetting ourselves, we stay in the stream of the direction we require. All we need to do is make sure that our mind remains smooth and undisturbed. The subject of meditation is like a magnet pulling our thoughts towards it. We simply become a part of the flow and in turn protect ourselves from disturbances. To master this art, one must eliminate conflicts and negativity in our being and direct our whole life towards good outcomes.

Air

The third state of attainment in yoga is known as *Samadhi* (union). In this state, our mind is like the nature of air, coming so close to the object of meditation that it takes on its very form. We arrive at a state of deep absorption, where only the essence of the place, object, or point shines forth in the mind. It's as if the mind was devoid of its own form, just as we do not see the air and only the light reflected from the object it surrounds. In this subtle state, we experience the object of meditation so deeply that there is often a state of confusion between the object of meditation and the meditator himself. This state is often accompanied by a feeling of bliss or amazing insights. To master this state, the practitioner will need to have achieved something very special. They need to master their inner desires and resolve any issues with the path of life, fate, and death. We need to be able to detach and let go of all worldly things at will, bringing all aspects of personality under control.

Fire

The fourth state of attainment is known by the yogis as *Samadhi* (without seed). In the Hermetic tradition, this state is known as becoming 'Aeon.' It relates to the element of fire or to matter in the form of energy. In this state, our consciousness is like radiating heat. We are like the radiating sun. We become whatever we choose, just like heat becomes one with the object it touches. The heat is not separate from the object but becomes part of the object it is within. In this state, we no longer have any confusion between self and subject. Only the subject and object of meditation exist. We are no longer meditating—we are becoming the subject of meditation. We have become the task, unhindered by any self or any objection. To master this advanced state, the practitioner must completely let go of all confusions in their perceived limitations of self. We must defeat vice and ignorance and embrace the true nature of who we are.

These are the four states of meditation that lead the practitioner on the path of harmony and balance towards enlightenment. The fifth state of attainment, far too complicated to be covered here, is a subtle state relating to the spirit which few living masters have experienced.

The History of Meditation

The art of meditation has been practised since antiquity. It has been a component in almost every spiritual and religious tradition across the world. It is unclear where the practice of meditation first began; however, it appears to have developed naturally throughout religious and spiritual traditions under a variety of different guises. I am sure the reader, however, will trust that there were civilizations that entered into varying states of meditation through the repetition of rhythmic chants and songs long before any written records in prehistoric times.

The first clear records of a formal and structured meditation practice are to be found in the Indian Hindu scriptures called the Vedas, a tradition dating back as far as 1500 BC[1]. This practice flourished, and by the fifth-century, meditation practices began to develop in China as part of the Confucian and Taoist traditions. Likewise, about this time the birth of Buddhism in India brought an entirely new focus to the contemplative art, whereby the aim from union with the divine shifted to that of understanding the true nature of self and interrelatedness with all things. By the eighth century, this form of meditation had moved from China to Japan, and thus the Zen tradition was formed. This Buddhist tradition primarily focused its attention on a seated form of meditation as an approach to life.

The Western world was not entirely devoid of a practice of its own. The ancient Egyptians gave reference to sacred 'sleep,' which was handed down to the philosophers of Greece, described as a form of meditation practice in the fourth century. This seems to have become part of the Abrahamic traditions along with Christianity, Islam, and Judaism with their own forms of meditations reflective of this tradition, including the use of repetition of

---

[1] Sagarika Dutt (2006). *India in a Globalized World*. Manchester University Press. p. 36. ISBN 978-1-84779-607-3.

certain god names, prayers, and postures. Indeed, the word 'meditation' originates from the Latin term *meditatio,* which means to contemplate or ponder upon.

The word *meditato* was first used with the meaning we would currently associate with meditation practice in the Christian tradition of contemplation, and by the fifth century was promoted by the Christian monk, St Bernard. However, over time the meaning changed and now has become associated with a variety of disciplines relating to serene reflection around the world. Meditation precedes and interpenetrates all world religions, traditions, and cultures. It is something that is valued by all and remains an untainted gift for mankind.

THE TRUE PURPOSE OF MEDITATION

CHAPTER 3

From a Hermetic point of view, you are a spark of pure goodness, a spirit so dedicated to the greater good for all beings that you have chosen to come into this world to help. From a Hermetic point of view, from a higher viewpoint of awareness, the human is dignified by the word, the ability to speak and to read. This higher nature is inherently connected with the sense of goodness.

Human beings are sent here to have good emotions, high intentions, and logical thought. You can see this goodness underlying in all human endeavours if you look carefully. We all have a sense of goodness that shines out in the most trivial of things. For example, if someone asks for help with something that is effortless or has little value, or if someone stops and asks for directions or asks for a light for a cigarette, there are very few people who would refuse this. We give naturally without thought or wish of something back. Likewise, you can see this goodness reflected in bigger situations such as emergencies, like if you are drowning or are in trouble, the car is stranded, or there is a medical emergency. We instantly call on the help of strangers who willingly oblige without a wish for payment or any negotiation or reward.

Hermetic philosophical belief is that this goodness should extend to all actions, and this is a natural way that man would function. His true purpose here on earth is to act as a form of caretaker or gardener, keeping things in balance and helping nature. The dreams of heaven that seem to be within each and every person, whether it be the Utopian Atlantis or Garden of Eden, are really the blueprints for how we know things should be.

The Hermeticists believe that the only sources of negativity or evil within a person are ignorance, confusion, pollution from some external source, or injury of someone.

To explain further:

1. Ignorance
   Ignorance is when people do not really know how things work. Maybe they have an ignorant idea of what will bring good outcomes for them and the people around them. Ignorance in the sense that they may have confused perceptions of who is part of the goodness and who is not. Or ignorance in a sense they do not have the skill to make things work.

2. Confusion
   Confusion can come in many forms. It's a frustration and emergency response when things do not work very well. Many people are hurting others or causing negative effects because they think they are defending themselves against an enemy that does not really exist.

3. Pollution
   Pollution comes in the form of external forces that get in the way of our expression of self. It could be said that if we are in a body, we have inherent difficulties to overcome. Overcoming these difficulties, limitations, character flaws, and external temptations are part of our challenge here.

4. Injury
   Sometimes this could be areas of the personality, body, or our own thought patterns that are not functioning in the way they are supposed to and require some degree of repair. Perhaps in the past, there were some hardships which caused an emergency response that limited your functioning, a bit like a spasm that closed down your emotions or cut off some memories. Could it be that something that happened injured you and healing is needed?

This means some form of therapy which slowly moves us towards the correct functioning of this aspect of the self. You may have noticed that a lot of the advice given to people as to what things should be done in any endeavour that leads to success tends to involve endevours that mimic the actions of those who are genuinely able to undertake the task with a positive, emotionally involved dedication. For example, if you are engaged in a business that you really love. No one needs to tell you to smile or help you with it. Likewise, someone enjoys an athletic pursuit; often their thoughts are better than someone who is not really wanting to do it. Hermetic meditation should be seen as tuning into genuine goodness within yourself. In this practice, we make sure that all aspects are in line with the inner and outer good.

CHAPTER 3: THE TRUE PURPOSE OF MEDITATION

Righteous Action

One of the best ways to start tuning in to the way things operate is to ensure that your actions are in harmony with a sense of goodwill for all. If you build a wall off balance, it is going to fall down, just as if you were to try to build a castle in the sand. Hermetic practitioners believe that a side effect of their meditation practice is that they will be able to see more clearly and act with more noble intentions.

A conscious effort to do good and skilfully apply your good intentions will also aid your meditation practice. In life, we want to succeed in the right way. Success follows from genuineness and a focus on noble deeds. Those that are in tune with the great good find the best allies and the best environments. The gifts of health, correct attitude, clear communication, and a truthful reflection of reality come to them.

Some people find that they can gain more particularity in material concerns if they find shortcuts that bully or subjugate others. From a Hermetic point of view, this is a poor replacement for working in-line and with the flow of your true nature and underlying good. In traditional Hermetic texts, there are often lists of vices that are replaced with virtues naturally. When examined, it becomes clear that often vices are tainted expressions of genuine wishes, wants, or even best wishes towards others. A firm, persistent dedication towards the best outcomes will reward any practitioner of Hermetic meditation in ways that cannot be expressed in words and allow them to drive out the four poisons mentioned above.

> *I engraved in myself the beneficent kindness of Poimandres and having been filled with what I desired; I was delighted. For the sleep of the body became the sobriety of the soul, the closing of the eyes became true vision, my silence became pregnant with the Supreme Good, and the utterance of the Word became the generation of riches. All this came to me who had received it from my Nous, that is to say from Poimandres, the Word of the Supreme. I have come, divinely inspired by the truth.*
>
> ~ The Corpus Hermeticum

BENEFITS OF MEDITATION

CHAPTER 4

If, from a Hermetic view, meditation is a practice of becoming at one with pure goodness, then what kind of manifestation of this blessing can we expect?

> What health benefits can you expect?
> How long do you have to practice before you can see the results?
> How often is it best to practice?

Over the last two decades, there have been over three thousand scientific studies on the benefits of meditation, including from such respected institutes as Harvard. Many of these studies are focused on specific types of meditation and indicate particular emotional effects, such as increased awareness, compassion, or social bonding. However, recent research has gone a long way to show how altering a person's state of mind can affect the body on a physical level and the health benefits this can bring.

Ten Benefits of Any Authentic Meditation Practice

1. Carmness
   The most powerful effect of consistent meditation practice is, rather predictably, inner calmness. This seems to be caused by the practice of learning to allow thoughts, no matter what they may be, to pass by while in meditation without attachment or response. By practising this skill, it seems to transfer into normal, everyday life, and thus has the benefit of allowing upsetting thoughts to occur without an overly negative response. This means that negativity is dealt with rather than dwelt upon.

2. Emotional Balance
It is generally observed that those who meditate demonstrate less neurotic behaviour and are balanced. They respond and adapt better to changes in life and to the emotional pressures these bring. When reading through study after study into meditation, it soon becomes clear that this could be a way to cure unhealthy emotional states such as anxiety, depression, or guilt. During meditation, it seems that the mind is cleansed, bringing about balance and emotional freedom.

3. Increased Immunity
Meditation has also been proven to boost immunity in recovering cancer patients. One study showed that when practised daily, meditation reduced the risk of breast cancer recurrence. Further studies have shown that regular practice boosts white blood cells in the elderly, giving them greater resistance to illness.

4. Improved Digestion
Studies have shown that those who practice meditation have far less incidence of digestive upset or heartburn. Meditation has also been shown to aid patients suffering from irritable bowel syndrome, in many cases proving better than most other forms of medication. Other studies show meditation as beneficial in dealing with other digestive problems, including diarrhoea, bloating, and constipation.

5. Lowers Blood Pressure
A study proved that meditation effectively lowered blood pressure when practised for several weeks. This appears to work by bringing around calmness and helping the body to become less responsive to stress hormones. This is similar to the way medication used to lower blood pressure works.

6. Anti-Inflammatory
Meditation has been clinically proven to lessen the symptoms associated with inflammation, arthritis, asthma, and some skin conditions such as psoriasis. This seems to work through stress reduction, as all the above problems typically worsen with increased stress, and so it follows that by helping reduce stress, the symptoms reduce also.

7. Reduction to the Risk of Heart Disease
Heart diseases are the biggest cause of death in the world.[2] Studies show that meditation is more effective in high-risk individuals than an exercise class. Regular meditation practice brings about a forty-eight percent reduction in a

---

[2] https://www.who.int/news-room/fact-sheets/detail/the-top-10-causes-of-death

heart attack or stroke. This seems to be caused by lower stress, decreased blood pressure, and a healthier outlook on life.

8. Increased Fertility
Studies show that women are more likely to conceive when practising meditation due to the calming effect on their mind and body. Likewise, it seems that the stress-reducing effect of meditation may also boost male sperm count and thus fertility.

9. Prevention of Obesity
Studies show that those who meditate have greater impulse control and so tend to eat a more balanced diet. The exact reason for this is not clear and could be due to several factors such as improved focus, a greater ability to ignore disturbances, or calming inner conflicts. This seems to be most apparent when looking at the person's eating habits. The change in their eating pattern seems to stem from their ability to prevent emotional eating, which in turn leads to an improved diet and prevents obesity.

10. Longevity Studies show that an essential part of human cells called telomeres, which determine how our cells age, are protected by meditation practice. Research is still in the early phases, but there is data from the University of California suggesting that,

Some forms of meditation may have salutary effects on telomere length by reducing cognitive stress and stress arousal and increasing positive states of mind and hormonal factors that may promote telomere maintenance.[3]

So, as you can see, meditation has great benefits and must be one of the best things you can do for your health. Studies show that many different types of meditation have very similar effects, but choosing a practice that you truly enjoy is probably the most likely to have the best effect. Most studies indicate that meditating for as little as twenty minutes a day for a few weeks is enough to bring associated health benefits.

---

[3] https://pubmed.ncbi.nlm.nih.gov/19735238/

HERMETIC MEDITATION – TUNING INTO THE GREAT GOOD

CHAPTER 5

Still the body

Fill your heart with kindness

Watch your breath like it's precious

Raise your awareness

Return to the true nature

As you have read earlier, meditation is a universal art. People practice meditation in varying ways and with different goals in mind. Many different traditions use the breath as the point of focus. Others imagine an image before them or repeat a mantra, such as Om or some form of prayer. This focus helps create a sense of unity in consciousness, where everything is moving in the same direction. How then does Hermetic meditation differ from these other methods?

Do you believe there is a force of goodness in the world? The Hermetic masters of old did, for the master there was always subtle force of good resonating within and underlying the whole of existence. It is this force that caused you to be born into the world. It is present within the energy of love expressed through your family and friends. When your cells were first dividing in the womb long before the development of the nervous system or brain formed, it was this great goodness that guided your body, formation, and growth. Even at this very moment, this goodness is all around you. It is that very same presence within the health and healing in your body. It is the awareness and understanding of your mind. It is the sunshine on the plants' leaves and the rainfall on the crops. The goodness fuses each seed to grow and to flourish. It is the light that allows you to see, the logic and correct thought in your mind—the guiding force behind your life's path.

- How do you become one with the great goodness?
- Have you ever noticed how small improvements have a cumulative effect?
- If you correct your posture, does your mood improve as well?
- If you spend time with positive people, do you feel refreshed and revitalised?
- Perhaps you have found doing something inspiring or artistic helps you function better. What about the effect of a good night's sleep?

The Hermetic practitioners of old were fully aware of this law of resonance and used it in their practice.

Goodness on All Levels

In the practice of Hermetic meditation, you aim to put everything into the ideal state of order. Think of this as manifesting goodness on all levels. When you sit, you do so with good posture, with your body in ideal alignment and harmony. This good posture naturally aids you in bringing goodness on other levels. Your breath becomes calm and regular. With your body in this restful rhythm fed with more oxygen, your awareness and consciousness rise. Your heart fills with good intentions and all are acting as one. When these are all in place, the good spirit will enter you. You will then tune in to all that is the light of the cosmos.

Higher Possibilities

The masters of old believed that by tuning into this goodness, amazing things could happen. When you and I tune in, the blessing will run through your very being, healing injuries, correcting errors or confusion, and bringing insight and understanding. In your material affairs, the goodness would also have an effect. It will bring skill and success to your workplace and make yourself a charged talisman, attracting goodness. Good people, good events, places, and objects would all move together. It was said that if groups sat in the awareness of the great good together, this effect would be magnified.

Oneness with the Great Good

Any practitioner who undertakes this discipline with consistent, ongoing practice will start to find the connection with the underlying force behind all that is. As everyone's experience of this is unique, and words tend to limit rather than aid the description, we will not go into too much detail here.

For many, this will start as a feeling of connection with all things or a sense of realisation that one's consciousness is far beyond the limitations previously experiencing. Others may find that they sense things or know things beyond themselves, as if the world is moving in their consciousness as thoughts. At some point in this unfolding, there will be a definite feeling. A sense of ecstatic union with a form of light. It's as if behind all things we find that awareness, beauty, kindness, and goodness are simply aspects of one force. Once you have felt this, your practice has changed. Lock in that feeling and hold on to it in your consciousness. From this moment onwards, your new practice is to tune into and be at one with the great good itself.

Purification

Once one is able to be at one with the light, then a process starts. A true initiation and a great realisation occurs. The practitioner will start to find themselves sitting in the luminance in a state of gentle ecstasy for considerable lengths of time. This process can feel heavenly at times, like an experience of pure beauty. Other times the practitioner may feel a slight sense of discomfort as they sit. This is a natural part of the process of purification and harmonisation taking place. The practitioner should be reassured that this is a great blessing but also be aware that for a while, compassion towards the self may be needed. This is because during their day to day life things are about to change. Any regrets, any confusion, or memories yet to be dealt with may start to surface. As consciousness evolves, we must let go of anything that holds us back. Let go of grudges, forgive yourself and others. Learn from your mistakes, learn to act with pure intentions, and function on a higher, more thoughtful level.

Illumination

If the practitioner is consistent and dedicated to their practice, then great evolutions will result. Every day when you sit in meditation, you are practising the ideal state of mind, and you are sitting in harmony with all things. With time this ideal state will start to become part of your daily functioning state of consciousness. The inner harmony you find will become outer harmony in your life. Your mind purified and lifted will be moved only by good intentions for all. Unfettered from limitations, you will be able to act skilfully and effectively in the world allowing all things to flourish. Then there will be a change in your meditation practice. Once you lifted yourself to the light, but now it shines through you as a light bringing healing and blessings to everything in your presence.

A More Modern Viewpoint

You do not need to believe in a separate divine force of pure goodness to practice Hermetic meditation. You just need to believe in cause and effect. That one good thing leads to another. Logical deductions lead to clear understandings. Clear, well thought out, and eloquent communication leads to better relationships. What goes around comes around. For this reason alone, it is very beneficial to practice putting everything in correct order though Hermetic meditation. To sit with a perfect posture, a calm breath, and a clear mind to bring these habits into daily life. Perhaps the knock-on effects of this kind of practice could seem like a miracle to some people.

This book is going to teach you how to sit in a calm and aware state and to 'tune into' this sense of goodness. Think of it as cultivating an attitude so positive that you naturally make the best of any situation. As you continue reading each chapter that follows, keep the idea of the 'great good' in mind and imagine how each small positive change could have a knock-on effect on everything else in your life.

HERMETIC PRINCIPLES FOR MEDITATION

CHAPTER 6

The Method of Hermetic Meditation Revealed

This chapter describes one of the most important meditation methods used by the original meditation practitioners. This would be the tradition that was handed down through the generations from ancient Egypt, all the way to the common era. In order to understand this technique, it is important to discuss some aspects of Hermetic philosophy. In order to do this, I would like to ask you to let go of any of your preconceptions of what meditation really is. To the Hermeticists, all things were made from pure consciousness. Everything you see, hear, smell, taste, or feel both internally and externally is a thought made manifest. All that varies is just how solid this manifestation is. So just as you form thoughts and ideas in your mind's eye, so too are all things formed.

To the Hermeticist, everything you see also originates from an original idea. A divine blueprint or template that defines the very qualities of that thing, species, invention, substance, or object. Behind all trees, there is an original spirit of the tree, the form of tree or idea of the tree from which they all radiate. Behind all humans, there is an archetype - an original concept of humanness. This realm of thoughts underlies all things and is in all things. All these thoughts exist in one big thought. This mind of the divine or big idea has had many different names throughout the ages. By the time the teachings the Hermeticists had written down had formed in the format in which we now receive them, they were calling it *To Agathos*—the great good, the divine goodness. The aim of Hermetic meditation is to become at one with this big picture—with this divine mind.

When the Hermetic practitioners were taking part in their incubation or meditation practices, they were not doing anything introspective. They were not watching their own thoughts or trying to clear their own mind—they were not focusing on their breath or repeating a mantra. Their aim was to step beyond the self. To let go of this limited idea and become one with the divine. To realize their own true divine nature. It was an expansive practice where you grasped your own divinity. In order to describe the core practice, the main method that Hermetic practitioners would have used to do this, I will reference the *Corpus Hermeticum*.

The first chapter of the *Corpus Hermeticum* is called *Poimandres*, and Poimandres is a corruption of an ancient Egyptian sentence that means the mind of Re or the mind of Ra, and you can see already that this is a clear indication that this chapter would describe the method of what I just laid out before you. Now for hundreds and hundreds of years, many thousands of people have read this beautiful description known as the 'Vision of Hermes', and they have read it as one man's enlightenment experience. But in those ancient times, they used to use this narrative as a means to describe techniques. This actual description describes the method used to achieve that enlightenment experience. Now, we are not going to cover the whole thing; we are going to cover the section that covers the actual technique. The practitioner that is being described is very experienced in meditation and because he achieves this sense of oneness, he goes on to have a great vision of the creation – the very method of the creation of the whole of everything. This would be considered the pinnacle achievement to occur after a lifetime of practice.

Let us step back to ancient Egypt, and the text begins:

Once, when my awareness became fixed on the things that are, my mind rose to a great height while my bodily senses became withdrawn as in sleep or when men are weighed down by too much food or fatigue of the body. Then I sensed a being of immeasurable proportion, and infinite dimensions spoke on to me.

Let's go through each one of these instructions in turn.

- *Once, when my awareness became fixed on the things that are.*

    To the original practitioner, this would be a clear reference to a technique that involved tuning into the big picture. This technique has been recorded covertly and overtly throughout history from ancient Egyptian times up until now, and that is something you see hinted at often in pre-Socratic Greek texts. To do this, you need to simply accept all things as one—all your senses, thoughts, and emotions. By accepting them all as one, by letting go of any difference between them, this allows you to start to tune into this big idea of where they all come from. This is a very powerful technique, and it takes practice to let go of the habitual separation of things.

CHAPTER 6: HERMETIC PRINCIPLES FOR MEDITATION

- *Then, my mind soared to a great height.*

You will find that through this practice, your awareness raises—you become very aware of everything internally and externally.

- *And my bodily senses sunk and withdrew.*

This stage is very commonly described in other meditation disciplines; this is the *Pratihara* of Yoga—withdrawal of the senses. In this case, the reasons by which senses start to withdraw is like a man who has eaten a lot or has grown very tired or someone who is going to sleep. He is going beyond his ideas or sense of self. He has stepped beyond himself, so his body is where he no longer resides. He is becoming a part of everything. He feels a sense of expansion of oneness. He knows he has achieved this goal.

- *Then I felt as if a being of immeasurable proportions and infinite dimensions spoke to me.*

This is about his oneness. We need to remember that in ancient times, words, thoughts, and any writing were all the same thing. We tend to reverse things. We tend to think of thinking as speaking to yourself. To them, speaking was thinking aloud. So, this is when he realized he achieved the goal, and he's become one with this *To Agathos*—this mind of God. The text goes on to describe a wonderful experience he has when he pictures in his mind's eye everything he wants to know, and because he's at one with this mind of God, he can see it. However, it does not describe the method of reversing the process. How do you come out of the meditation? This would be very obvious to the Hermetic practitioner of the day—you were expected to work it out yourself. Instead of resting your mind on all the things that are, you would start resting your mind, would tune back into your body and each one of your senses, then reopen them and separate things so you could bring yourself back to your normal state.

This is the basic technique of Hermetic meditation. Of course, there are many other special skills, all of which I hope in the future to bring back for you. For many years people have believed there has not been a Hermetic or Western meditation lineage, but that's not true. The reason it seems non-existent is it has never been presented in a modern, understandable way like the Eastern teachings have. I believe it is time for these techniques to come back in order to bring balance to the world.

As Above So Below

In order to get the most from our meditation practice, we need to approach it in a positive, honest, and exact way. In order to do this, let us consider the Hermetic rule *As Above So Below*.

You should consider your meditation practice as a daily joy. Meditation practice is a sunlamp on your soul just as sunlight hits a plant and the plant gains great nutrition from this and can grow. Your meditation practice helps unfold hidden talents, beauties, and blessings within yourself, so it should be embraced with joy. It is time just for you. Allow yourself expression in this work to your full potential and majesty. The feel it should have is the same kind of feel you see in people when they are doing something they really love and engage with. You are like the astronomer adjusting the telescope to bring things into focus so you can behold the celestial beauty. You are like the flower arranger putting nature's gift in just the right position. The artist's brush, the writer with a pen, the sculptor with their hands. This sense of joy shows full engagement and full engagement is what you seek.

How you practice your meditation will affect how you live your life. During your meditation practice, you are practising the ideal state of consciousness. The state of consciousness that will create ripples in your normal waking state of consciousness. So, if you want to live with joy, practice with joy. If you want to perfect the art of life, perfect your meditation practice. Going into your meditation with this attitude will really help your performance and bring the right quality naturally to the forefront. That would be the quality of being exacting.

The Posture

When you sit, consider your body and mind as one. All positions of your body and all movements of your body are the same as the positioning of your mind and the thoughts that you engage with. Make sure your posture is correct. You may need to observe yourself in order to find what postural habits you have that need to be changed and transformed. Have a look at daily life and see what is happening. Your posture could be affected by the following:

- If you are working on a computer where you are hunched over, and your neck is stiff and bending forwards.

- If you are so goal-centred that you tend to be seeking the reward or the results, this can also encourage the movement of the head leaning forward.

- Perhaps you are introspective, so you tend to look down when meditating.

- Maybe you have tension and feel that it is bringing your shoulders into a concave position.

Have a look for imbalances in your day to day life, such as if one shoulder is higher than the other. Is tension holding you in a certain position? Then in your meditation, take to form the ideal posture, bringing everything into alignment. Know that your posture changes your mood.

It is far better to be gentle with this because your mind and body need time to get used to this different way of being. Remember that five minutes of sitting in a state of unbroken meditation in the ideal posture is better than sitting for five hours when you are enforcing the very habits that need to be changed.

The Breath

Now, I mentioned the positioning of your body reflects your consciousness, and this is most certainly true. Your breathing shows the quality of your thoughts. Make sure your breathing is relaxed on the abdomen and slightly deeper than usual. The movements of your body are also movements of the mind because your body is driven and controlled by the mind. For this reason, put yourself in a particular ritual posture or mudra. Remain in that posture. Do not switch around. When you are switching around your body posture, you are switching around your focus. This is not good practice. You may find that certain postures take some dedication to maintain. This has meaning you should contemplate and shows an area you should refine. Likewise, view any movement or change as real; for example, if you open your eyes and close them again, this is a disturbance. It shows your vision is wavering. Make sure that you keep your eyes horizontal and your nose vertical. Consider yourself as a builder with a plumb bob and a level. This means you have a balanced body and a balanced inner vision. You are upright in your focus and upright in your vision. Once you have set your timer and you can see that your meditation timer is counting down, then place it somewhere out of sight and keep your mind fully on the meditation. Any excuse to glance at the meditation timer is a disturbance and should be avoided.

During your practice, you want to record your success and the degree of the disturbances that you have fastidiously because you want to keep improving and evolve your consciousness. Have a string of beads a mala or rosary, and if you think about something off-topic or lose concentration, then move your finger to the next bead. If you are attempting to clear your mind of all thoughts, you can use the same method. At the end of the mediation, when the timer goes off, you can see how many disturbances you had. Record that in your diary or put it on a chart. As the days, weeks, months, and years go by, you will see the strength of your concentration and the purity of your consciousness forms as the count of beads becomes less and less. Only with this fastidious method of control over your practice will you keep making progress.

Now, during your meditation, there will be some opportunities to overcome the weaknesses or shortcomings you have in the day to day life. These will present themselves. When you sit, if you find tension forming in the body, use your breath and, on the outbreath, release that tension. Take this as an opportunity to cultivate inner tranquillity in the mind and tranquillity in the body. You want to let go of this tension, and this will start to permeate into your daily life. If you find yourself wanting to move from some small disturbance or scratch an itch, this as an opportunity to cultivate impartibility and self-control. This will mean that in day to day life, you will be able to hold your tongue when words would not be useful. Or not get involved in something that you cannot bring a positive influence towards. You will find it easier to endure things that are necessary to achieve your goals and to remain balanced. By using every possible disturbance to train yourself, you will cultivate this exacting quality, and honesty will start to shine forth.

Often you see people find ways to make meditation easier for them with excuses. They will not turn their phone off, and when the phone rings, they have an excuse to break off their meditation training and rob themselves of the time to improve. Sometimes they will replace meditation training with observational training of something entertaining, or they will bring a drink or some other stimulus into the circumstance of their training. They do this in order to change the exercise rather than change themselves.

Remember, you want to raise your consciousness and improve your ability to meet the standards of meditation, not lower the standards. These are the principles you need to apply using the standards *As Above So Below* to bring great success to your meditation and let it flourish in your life. There is a specific exercise you can use to make sure all of the benefits I have described are installed within you.

1. Place before you a mirror so that when you sit, you can see the whole of your body.
2. Set your posture as perfectly as possible using the mirror as a guide
3. Relax your breathing
4. Keep your eyes open and use your own image as the focus of your meditation.

Do so with a sense of kindness that you want everything that is good for this person and want to fully understand the image before you. Consider what you are looking at as the greatest symbol of meditation. Greater than any mandala, religious symbol, or mantra. Get used to really looking at yourself. Use this time to adjust your physical posture and also your inner posture. Keep your emotions positive and any negative criticism or doubt that comes forth consider as an opportunity for transformation. Take it and turn it to the ideal expression. This is a very beautiful practice and should be approached with a sense of reverence and joy. Start very small and work up until you are able to sit with a perfect posture inside and out. As *Above So Below* and continue unbroken for 30 minutes. Then you will know that all the lessons stated here are in your possessions and your true qualities.

Creating a Space for Meditation Practice

The first step in starting your meditation practice is, if possible, to create a conducive environment. This is to say, to make room for your practice, both in terms of physical space but also in terms of time and focus.

The following section addresses the foundation of how to set up a lifestyle, ethos, and indeed an entire environment for self-improvement, which will enforce your continual improvement in meditation. This book is primarily focused on meditation, but these principles can be applied to any skill or any form of discipline.

First Principal – Joy

This principle relates to the importance of enjoying what you do. This can be witnessed in terms of making the mental space for your practice. Going into practice with a correct attitude makes a vast difference to your practice and is the most influential aspect. Your meditation practice should be approached as a thing to savour and enjoy rather than a hardship to endure and just get through.

If you find that you are not enjoying the practice of meditating, you will only feel resistance, and it will be counterproductive to achieving the goal. It is important to enjoy the practice. If you do not, a change of attitude is required. Without a sense of enjoyment, it is hard to fully engage. You can become focused on results instead of the practice. Any tenseness means that effort is holding you back, not pushing you forwards. For this reason, it is important to keep a sense of daily joy, and you may need to change the approach to the exercises. Perhaps view it as a game, or maybe see the process as a spiritual dedication. Perhaps think of meditation as you are not doing it for yourself, but for a higher power. This can take the pressure off and start progress again. Search to find whichever method you find to reignite that joy.

Second Principal – Environment

The ideal place to sit is underneath a tree or in nature, but if that is not possible, make sure there are beautiful pictures that inspire you and consider incense that uplifts the soul while you practice—perhaps listening to music before your practice. Make sure your environment is clean and tidy. Reflect your goals with objects that are in harmony with what you are trying to do.

Creating a Sacred Space

Great importance has been placed within many spiritual traditions upon the significance of creating a sacred space. We may observe that many spiritual traditions honour this and create a sacred place for practice. One of the reasons is that over time a charge of energy is formed, which can further aid you in your practice. Another reason is that it focuses the mind, as we know when we enter a sacred place for practice.

If possible, clear out that junk room and decorate it according to your tastes. Maybe use a soft neutral colour that feels soothing and calming. If that is not possible, perhaps section off an area of your bedroom or in a room that is dedicated to where you can practice. Make that area a reminder and dedicated space to the practice of meditation by placing inspiring images of people or places that represent your goals. These items create an elevated state to motivate you as you aspire towards improvement.

Creating an Atmosphere Through the Senses

As mentioned previously, we can use a visual aid through the use of inspiring images or even use candles for added atmosphere. Another method is the use our olfactory senses through smell. Perhaps burning incense or aromatherapy oils to help prepare us. Over time an association is formed between the scent and practice, which also acts as a reminder whenever we smell that particular scent; we know it is time to practice.

Another method people like to use is auditory. Listening to beautiful music before practice is a great way to prepare the body and mind for the exercise. Some people like to use a mantra to aid them in a single focus and create a conducive mind for meditation.

Creating a Peaceful Environment

If the environment where you live is not harmonious, then it is very difficult to achieve the goal of meditation. When starting out, it is important to find a quiet and restful place to practice. Perhaps we live in a demanding and busy household where this is a challenge. If so, try to find a quiet time when you know there will be fewer disturbances. Perhaps practice early in the morning before the family members get up or late at night when everyone has gone to bed. However, if there is conflict in your home, you will need to move towards resolving this, as it will only impede upon your meditation practice. All these suggestions can all be incorporated into a ritual to prepare for practice.

Third Principal - Inspiration

It is important to ask yourself the question, 'Are you still inspired by this goal?'

If not, go and find your inspiration where you left it. Think back to the last book you read, the film you watched, or the person you spoke with who inspired you, and this will reignite your inspiration. Inspire yourself with art, reading, study, or with friendly conversation in these areas. In the future, watch carefully for any lulls in inspiration, and in particular, protect yourself against them. And finally, the light of a teacher or guru. This may not be a literal teacher but a source of teaching that inspires you and lifts you up on an ongoing basis.

CHOOSING A MEDITATION POSTURE

CHAPTER 7

Progressive Meditation Postures for Beginners and More Advanced Practitioners

The body is the easiest thing to adjust. Good posture has a positive effect on all other levels.

A Guide to Good Posture

Getting the right posture is indeed very important since having the correct posture also affects our mental functioning. There is a tendency for us to slump, and this habit is partly due to the fact we are often bent over working on a computer or at a desk.

The Three Vases

With all the seated postures, the hips must be angled correctly. An analogy that may be of use is to imagine the body as three vases holding water. The first vase is in the hips. Make sure they are straight. Imagine that in the centre of your pelvis is a vessel holding water. Once the hips are in place, then the rest of the body falls into better alignment. The second vase is the chest area. Using the same visualization of a vessel holding water, imagine the water becoming level, as we straighten and angle ourselves correctly. The third vase is the neck and head. Make sure the chin is tucked in. There is a tendency for us to push our necks forward. You can even imagine a bowl of water on top of your head. These tips can be applied to all postures.

Four Main Progressive Meditation Postures

Listed below are Four main progressive postures from beginner meditation postures to more advanced demonstrations for those wishing to progress to the lotus position.

1. Throne posture
2. Easy pose
3. Burmese posture
4. Half lotus
5. Full lotus

These postures can be practiced anywhere and do not need any special attire. They provide gradual progression from sitting in a chair to the more advanced poses, such as the lotus posture. The initial postures are great for people who are just beginning. Each posture can be practiced until the body adjusts to each stage. Starting with the easy pose, graduate to the Burmese posture, and finally practice the full lotus posture.

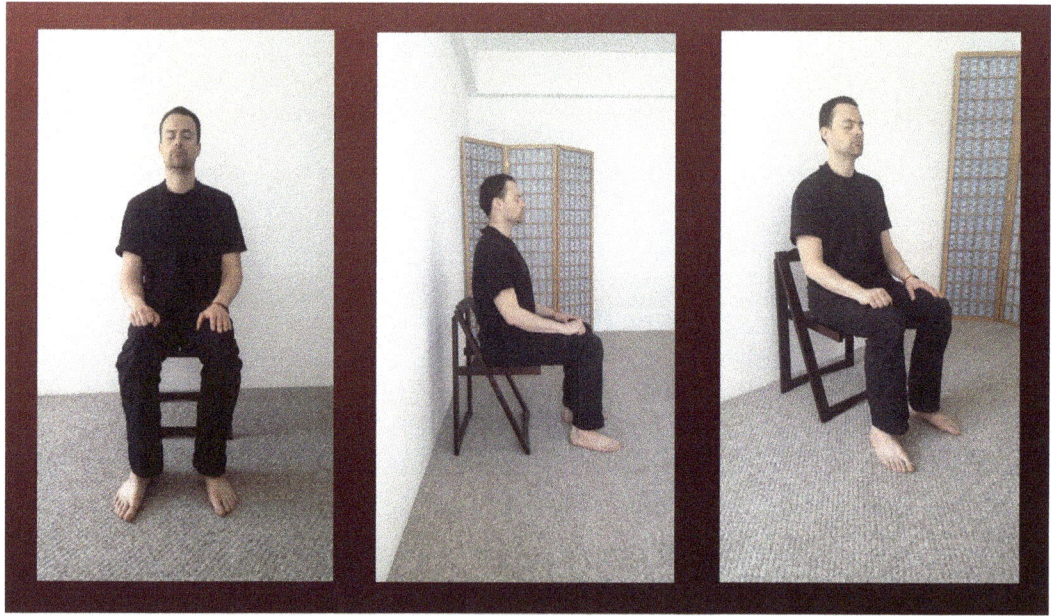

Figure i: The Throne Posture

Throne Posture

This posture is known as the Egyptian Throne posture due to its origin. This posture is excellent for those who have a medical condition that prevents them from sitting cross-legged or have a spinal injury that restricts their movement. A benefit of this pose is it enables one to meditate in public when travelling or when sitting, ow when waiting in a lengthy queue. With this posture, it is essential to keep the spine straight and use the support muscles to keep the back erect and away from the back support of the chair. Feet are planted on the ground, and hands rested on top of the knees (see fig.1).

The throne posture is the ideal position for your meditation practice. It's well worth learning to utilize this position even if you've mastered other poses. It allows you to sit for long periods without any hardship to your body so you may entirely focus on finding the exact state of mind or achieving your particular goals. Likewise, it's a very unassuming meditation posture. If you want to practice your meditation in public, you can do so without drawing any attention to yourself. The throne posture is usually associated with Western traditions, but you may be surprised at how often it's used in the East. I'm going to share traditional wisdom in terms of symbolism and practical advice from the ancient Egyptian and Greek lineages.

In ancient Egyptian, the word for throne is Isis, and the goddess Isis is the mother goddess who represents all goodness and good intentions. You can see that the hieroglyph of her name, which is often on her head, is a throne. No one knows why she was named after a throne, but I believe it's because she was born from the love between Geb, the Earth, and Nut, the sky. To an ancient Egyptian, where most people would be sitting on the floor, a chair had a special significance. Being the point between Heaven and Earth, it is the posture of complete balance, where you have higher inspiration and vision from the sky and the grounded reality from the earth beneath your feet. In honour of the goddess Isis, I believe it's very good for someone to start their meditation practice by keeping in mind the good intentions and positive outcomes they're trying to create.

Now how do we know about the ancient Egyptian use of the throne posture so many centuries ago? We know from the statues they created and from the depictions they had in their temples. We also have some direct knowledge through the Hermetic schools who would have probably learned from the same statues we are looking at and possibly from the Egyptian priests remaining at the time. The Hermeticists have a saying, 'As above, so below'. When we start our practice, we do need to keep this in mind. Our physical posture is what creates our mental posture for our meditation. The ancient Egyptians used to sit with their feet and knees together, so it's vital if you're a man to make sure everything is comfortable when you do this. This was an important and symbolic gesture for the Egyptians as well as a practical posture for us.

In ancient Egypt, the builder's square being at right angles, represented Maat, the personification of truth, justice, and correctness. You need a correct body to have a correct mind, so make sure your thighs are always horizontal. You can do this by putting blocks under your feet or lifting them on cushions or by sitting on a cushion yourself. Whenever possible, make sure things are well-aligned. If you fail to do this or are at a slight angle, you will find your knees are lower than your hips at the edge of the chair. This will cut off the blood flow, and then your meditation becomes an exercise in imperturbability rather than higher awareness or mindfulness.

Once you know this area of your body is in alignment, make sure your pelvis is straightened and your back is straight. You will probably notice that on ancient Egyptian statues they always had one fist clenched, possibly holding an Ankh or some symbol, and one open. This, I believe, was an allusion to the rod of polarity, just like the signs we see with the crook and the flail. It was a sign of male and female, light and dark, active and passive. This is a sound symbol of balance, which we can combine with our thoughts on the throne itself.

The Egyptian statues likewise always have the head perfectly in alignment, with the shoulders back and looking straightforward, as if into the distance. When you first start with your throne posture, make sure you gradually increase the time that you're sitting. You will see the statues often seated with their back against the chair, but in modern Hermetic practice, you will mostly see people supporting their own back. This prevents you from losing awareness and becoming sleepy. Sometimes you will see some beads being held. I've seen this on an Egyptian statue with the bead string to the side of the knee and outside the thigh. I have also seen Phocean statues which are imitative of Egyptian states, with longer beads hanging over the elbow. It may be that they sometimes used rosaries or malas when they were timing their meditation. If you read the Hermetic texts, it appears they were more focused on meditation as an exercise as we would practice a physical exercise now trying to achieve a state of mind and holding it for as long as comfortable rather than timing it.

If we look to Christian monasteries in the Egyptian Coptic Orthodox Greek tradition, they have a lineage of the throne posture, which dates back to the pre-Socratic Greek philosophers, and they sit slightly different. For them, the knees are always apart. They mostly use a rosary that is strung over the knee to encircle it as a wreath. This is a beautiful way to practice. Sometimes you'll see them hold this over their heart as one would hold their hand over their heart for an oath or a pledge. Likewise, you'll see there are some small variations in how they utilize the posture. Often, they will use a cushion and this cushion is put on the back of the throne so that when you sit you're slightly off the edge. This naturally straightens the pelvis and is useful when you're first beginning, as it puts you in perfect alignment.

In some of the monasteries and ancient meditation temples I visited in Greece and southern Italy, you can see the cushion is built into the chair. If we go further up the body, you'll see everything else is a bit more relaxed. The spine is not always straight, maybe relaxed forward, and the head is tilted forward. This probably comes from a tradition of keeping the focus on the navel. In modern Christianity's *Hesychia*, known as inner silence practice, this pose is interpreted as a position of reverence or prayer. This is very interesting because if you read the ancient Indian texts, you'll find all the modern postures we associate with meditation involve tilting the head forward as if gazing downward and through the thighs or lap.

By drawing from these two beautiful traditions and adding to your practice with the small adjustments and tips mentioned, you will be able to build your own throne posture position. This posture will help you perfect your inner self and thus be able to bring good works into the world. Many people have added symbolism to the throne itself. In Hermeticism, the four legs of a chair have become associated with earth, air, fire, and water, or with the vows, 'To know, to will, to dare, and to stay silent.' There are beautiful Christian texts which go through the different areas of a throne, associating each part of its physical construction with a different virtue. Likewise, in the Bible, there is an association with the word throne and an order of celestial beings, or angels, which represent the divine authority.

CHAPTER 7: CHOOSING A MEDITATION POSTURE

Everyone can find their own associations with the physical chair to suit their personal taste. The most important thing is to be able to make this posture comfortable for your body so you can do your inner work with ease.

Easy Pose

Do not be afraid to use props to make your sitting time more comfortable. You can use folded blankets or a special meditation cushion, sometimes called 'zafu'. This is especially good for the lotus posture variations as it helps keep your knees lower than your hips. However, ensure that it is a low cushion. You want your knees to descend toward the floor, but you do not want to overwork the forward tilt of your pelvis.

In yoga, this is named 'easy posture' and in ancient Egypt, you can see scribes sitting in this position for their writing. This pose can be performed anywhere with little flexibility and is the basic cross-legged posture.

Figure ii: Easy Pose

Progressions Within the Easy Pose

Figure iii: Using the wall for support.

Figure iv: Use of a cushion.

When starting, this posture may be difficult to perform for any length of time if the hips are not flexible, and the back muscles are not used to supporting the body in that way. Using a wall allows the back to be supported. The hips sink down and gradually open up while allowing the back to be still supported. In the beginning, the recommended time to start with is five minutes. You may build up to thirty minutes. Once you have practised the easy pose for a few weeks with your back against the wall and can sit for fifteen or twenty minutes of meditation, it is time to move to the second progression.

Figure v: Using the foot as a support.

Due to the nature of our lives, our hip flexors are often very tight and need time to release. Due to this reason, sitting in this position on the edge of a cushion can be of great benefit. The function being, as mentioned above, to allow the hips to align themselves correctly and the knees to sink lower than the hips. This corrects the tilt in the pelvis. There is a tendency to slump when we sit cross-legged, so placing a cushion on the edge of our seated position allows us to sit up straight.

As you can see, I am using one heel and one foot to support my legs in this posture. This also aids stability when sitting.

Extending the Arms

As you can observe in the demonstrations for this posture, my arms are extended out straight to reach my knees. Often when starting, it is necessary to do this because the arms act as a stabilizing balance.

General Posture Alignment

Imagine your chin is slightly tucked under, and there is a string pulling at the centre of your head so that you are sitting up nice and straight. Your hips should be angled so that your back maintains its natural curve. The most common problem area is to slouch. We want to make sure that our pelvis is horizontal and not tilted. This means using a cushion is very useful for this purpose. You can sit just on the edge of the cushion so that it naturally straightens the tilt in the pelvis.

Second Progression Easy Pose

The second stage in the easy pose posture progression is to sit away from the wall and use your back muscles for support. Just three to five minutes to begin with. You will find that like any form of physical training, it takes a while for your body to adapt. You may also find that your mind rebels to the stillness and you need to keep your focus on the subject of meditation. This is all good and part of the progress. As your flexibility improves and your meditation increases in duration, you may consider the next progression, which is the Burmese posture. However, it is advisable to wait until you have reached fifteen or twenty minutes of meditation in the easy pose before you move on. For those who are already flexible in the easy pose, it is fine to move on if they so wish.

3. Burmese Posture

Figure vi: Burmese posture

This is one of the best meditation postures in existence. For years I was using more complicated postures and found that after long periods my legs were numb. I also found it a challenge since I often had to meditate when travelling or due to time restrictions did not have sufficient time to warm up. This posture was recommended to me by a Japanese master who informed me that this posture is prevalent in Zen practice. This is a simple posture to master compared to the lotus posture and will be of use to you for the rest of your life. It also stretches the hips and opens them in preparation for the lotus posture. In this posture, the legs are not crossed, and the knees are turned outwards to the floor. The legs are bent, and the feet are placed in front of the pelvis, with one foot in front of the other. Make sure that your heels are more or less in alignment. It is good to warm up and spend a few minutes stretching before sitting in this posture. Let your hands rest at the top of the thighs or on the heels. Feel free to adjust the position of the feet until you are comfortable. It is perfectly acceptable to either have the feet straight in front of each other or to let them pass so that one foot is next to the other ankle. You may also have to adjust the angle to allow you to place your calves or knees on the floor.

In the Burmese posture, you must pay attention to keeping your legs on the floor. When you cross your legs in full or half lotus it naturally pushes the knees down. Not so with the Burmese posture. It may take a while for you to sit comfortably in this position. To begin with, you may not be able to rest your legs down comfortably. Do not worry about this, as you will find that this improves as the course progresses.

If you are already practicing meditation, I advise you to convert to the Burmese posture to help prepare yourself for the lotus posture.

When practicing twice a day, it is recommended that you vary which foot is at the front of each knee so that the hips adjust in both positions. Therefore, balance is maintained and a bad habit is not formed by only sitting in one way. In this posture, it is also recommended to wear loose clothing to allow greater movement in flexibility. Once this posture is comfortable to sit in for up to twenty to thirty minutes, and once you can sit in ease, then you will be able to advance to half lotus.

4. Lotus Posture

Half Lotus

Figure vii: Half lotus posture

Sit with your legs straight out before you. Sit on a cushion or folded mat to elevate the hips and allow the knees to sink through hip rotation. Keeping the back upright, bring your right leg into the cradle stretch position and externally rotate the right hip. Keep the right foot flexed. This helps to prevent rotation at the knee and ankle joints. Place the right foot on top of the left thigh.

Relax the whole right leg. Now slowly bend the left knee in towards the folded right leg. Cross the leg in front of you. Pick up your left foot and lower shin and gently lift it onto the right thigh. You have now completed the pose. The left knee may be slightly above the floor. Relax. With practice, this will even up.

Sit in a balanced upright position. The ideal position is not hard to find. Just watch your breathing and position yourself where it is most free and easy. Either rest the hands on the knees with the palms facing up or hold them together on your lap. Start by staying in the pose for brief periods, increasing your stay as your hips increase in flexibility. When your legs grow tired, stretch them straight out before you and gently massage your knees. Cross your legs the other way around and practice on the other side.

Full Lotus

Figure viii: Full lotus posture

Sit with your legs straight out before you. Sit on a cushion or folded mat to elevate the hips and allow the knees to sink through hip rotation. Keeping the back upright, bring your right leg into the cradle stretch position and externally rotate the right hip. Keep the right foot flexed. This helps prevent rotation at the knee and ankle joints. Place the right foot on top of the left thigh.

Relax the whole right leg. Now slowly bend the left knee in towards the folded right leg. Cross the leg in front of you. Pick up your left foot and lower shin and gently lift it onto the right thigh. You have now completed the pose. The left knee may be slightly above the floor. Relax. With practice, this will even up.

Sit in a balanced upright position. The ideal position is not hard to find. Watch your breathing and position yourself where it is most free and easy.

Either rest the hands on the knees with the palms facing up or hold them together on your lap. Start by staying in the pose for brief periods, increasing your stay as your hips increase in flexibility.

When your legs grow tired, stretch them straight out before you and gently massage your knees. Cross your legs the other way around and practice on the other side.

Benefits of the Lotus Pose

- Strengthens the back
- Improves posture
- Invigorates the entire nervous system
- Improves circulation between the legs and torso
- Increases circulation in lumbar area and abdomen
- Calms the mind
- Aids digestion and peristaltic movement
- Increases circulation to abdominal organs
- Best meditation posture, as it provides the classical sitting position for longer periods of time without bodily movement
- Promotes great mobility of the ankles, knees, and hips

Through our meditation, we are seeking inner calmness, stillness, and evolution of our state of consciousness. The posture we chose is not as important as the mental posture we maintain. I have met great masters of meditation who simply sit in the throne posture in a chair, just like you see with the Egyptian Pharaohs doing. That is quite a flexible posture to practice and it allows you to sit in a park or on a train to perform your exercises without drawing attention to yourself.

The benefit of following a progressive posture training is that you will able to sit anywhere in nature without restriction. To practice all of them in succession will aid not only in greater flexibility but allow us to meditate anywhere.

Gymnastics or Yoga and Meditation

In the ancient temples of Egypt and Greece, gymnastics were considered part of the healing art of meditation practice. Specific healing temples had gymnasiums where exercises were performed under prescription to bring goodness in the form of health back to visitors. To perform gymnastic postures in a Hermetic way, take a few moments to contemplate health and relaxation, bringing yourself to the right positive state of mind before practicing them.

Make sure you practice consists of seven postures that flow together beautifully with a sense of elegance and beauty. Practice breathing in smooth, gentle breaths that go all the way down to your feet and back up to the top of your head. Watch your breath as if it is precious and let your mind calm. As you adjust your body, use elegant precision. Use the practice as a means to dwell in awareness and let the alignment of your body align you with all that is good and healthy. Every Hermetic practitioner can find his or her own routine. There are many books both from the East and the West that contain yoga or gymnastic postures. The exchange of posture and exercises between the East and West has been ongoing since Alexander the Great. In the modern-day, we should feel very grateful to the practitioners from India who have restored these exercises to their rightful place. We should have no resistance to learning from their wisdom in this art. Health and physical fitness are physical manifestations of the Good, of the alignment, and of the success which we wish to amplify into our practice, With this principle in mind, we can be guided in our quest for good seated postures. Those who seek a specific routine for good posture are recommended to purchase my book, Becoming the Lotus.

HOW TO MEDITATE

CHAPTER 8

A Detailed Method of Hermetic Meditation

1. Posture

   The first step is to establish good posture in both terms of body and mind. Think of this as the very first stage of dwelling in goodness. Using principles outlined earlier, take time to consciously arrange your body into proper posture with calm, care, and enjoyment. Move towards the best possible posture. Without being too much of a perfectionist, use your body as a guide and work with it. The posture should feel comfortable and have a positive, uplifting effect. Good posture leads to raised awareness and a good mood. Place your hands on your thighs, and with your palms up close your eyes and take a few moments just to breathe and allow your body to be in comfort. Command your entire being to relax. You can just sit and let the natural process of the seat of the right posture unfold. If you like, you can work with it and take a few moments just to picture your whole body in perfect posture and all the functioning of your body in perfect order. Let health flow through you and harmony form inside.

2. Breath

   Now move your attention to your breath. You may have noticed that it has naturally slowed. Perhaps your breathing is from your abdomen now. Watch your breath like it's precious. Allow it to become smooth, slow, and long. Your breathing pace should be calming and feel natural. The mind naturally follows your breathing, so it's worth taking some time to let your awareness rest on the breath.

Move your focus to your breath. Let the whole process of breathing continue without the strain of any conscious control. Just be present, feeling the breath as it flows in and out of your being. Keep your awareness on the sensation, sound, and rhythm of your breath. Become a calm, unattached witness to the process, joyfully observing the sensation of the breath moving.

Don't feel a need to control the breath. Let your mind be at one with the breath and let the breath be as it will. You may find that at times the pace of your breathing changes. This is all part of the process. Learn to make this part of the natural process. Just observe and experience it. The breath is naturally long when we are relaxed and short when we need to let go of tension. Watch the pace of life with pure awareness, which is your true nature.

3. Expand your Awareness

Let the whole of your body relax. Enjoy just being there and letting the body relax at its own natural pace. You may notice that although your focus has been on your breath, your awareness, in general, is starting to increase. Watch as your body awareness grows and how your mind starts to be present to each sensation of the body. Soon you will find your mind naturally begins to clear. Watch as this sensation spreads and magnifies. You are now entering a state of meditation. Let your mind rest gently on every thought or sensation. If your focus starts to move to anything in particular, bring it back to the whole, really embody every sense, sound, smell, or other input as one. View everything as a calming, healing blessing, and gift.

4. Tune in

As you sit in a state of calm natural awareness, with practice, you will discover the innate ability you have to raise your consciousness and expand your sense of self. The feeling should be a joyful connection to the job in hand, similar to the feeling you get from a pure focus on a hobby or when you are fully engaged in something enjoyable. With practice, you will find you gain a better ability to increase your receptiveness to outside and inner sensations. We all have a limited degree of control over our level of awareness. When asked to concentrate with some effort, we can increase our focus. With Hermetic meditation, we find our awareness volume control and learn how to increasingly turn it up under our control.

Accept inner and outer sensations as one. Expand your sense of self and allow a feeling of oneness with everything. Let all pass without attachment or need to interact. Sometimes you may feel in harmony or at one with the goodness resonating, or nature itself. At times of healing or rebalancing, the breaths may be of unequal length. That is to say, the in breath and out breath may have different durations or intensity. Whatever the breath needs to be, let it be natural and unforced. Relax, focus, and just observe and experience it.

5. Sending Good Wishes to Others (Optional)

Using this method you can use your link with the great good to bring blessings to others. As you feel ready to come out of your meditation state, simply let your mind slowly go back to its normal state. Slowly let your body wake up and start to move. At this point, you may choose to take a moment to send a good wish to a person or place that you feel could benefit from tuning in with the goodness and clear vision that you have just embodied in your practice.

To do this, imagine forming before you a beautiful shimmering silver disk, almost like the moon floating before you. Then imagine the person you feel could benefit from a blessing or healing pictured on that disk. Picture clearly in your mind's eye with the best possible intent the ideal outcome of the situation which comes to mind. If you choose to do this, then once you have expressed your kind intentions, move your mind away from the subject immediately and get on with your daily business.

6. Progressing in Your Meditation

With practice, you will find some beautiful changes as a result of your meditation practice. In daily life, you will be more calm, carefree, and adaptable. Your ability to focus, recover, and enjoy life will be renewed. With time your breath will transform in parallel with your mind. Your breathing will slow down and become more subtle and refined. Sometimes your breath can even seem to have stopped. At such times you will experience a wonderful sense of calmness, oneness, and inner peace.

7. Remember: You Already Know How to Do This

Hermetic meditation is something natural, relaxed, and innate. It's not something you need to learn—it's something you need to remember. There are moments in your life when you have been in a place of beauty and taken a few moments to just 'soak in' the scene. It could be from a long walk in nature where you stood for a few moments to look out over a lake or valley. Some people find the same awareness and serenity sitting in the garden or from a classical concert or work of art.

So, don't overthink it. Remember that time when you just sat on a tree stump and just sat? Cast your mind to times in life that allowed your mind to feel clear, free from the worries of the world, and at one with everything for a few minutes around you. You are sure to have experienced it. It's a natural part of life and happens to all of us now and again. With daily practice, you can develop this ability to a very high degree.

Some Queries Addressed Regarding Experiences During Meditation Practice

1. Why do I get hot in meditation?

I would like to discuss an interesting phenomenon that happens to some people who meditate. It's something that can start to happen when you first learn to meditate, or it's something that can appear later on in your meditation practice. The phenomenon I'd like to talk about is that of increased body temperature. Many people experience this like a fever, and when they start their practice, it comes on associated with sweat, making it difficult for them to focus. Other people experience this as a dry heat centralized in different points on the body, and sometimes it can be so strong there is actual physical pain.

I'm going to cover the different possible causes of this heat and how you should deal with it. The first possible reason for this increased body temperature is that your technique needs to be improved. When we practice meditation, we are looking to use the whole of our mind and consciousness in a harmonious and integrated way. Our meditation improves from cultivating our level of consciousness and purity of focus. This results in the whole more powerful than the sum of its parts.

When some people practice meditation, they lean on the most potent part of their mind. So, if someone is very imaginative, they can use their imagination to force an extra gear into place so that their practice is temporarily improved. Maybe someone who is very emotional can engage a strong sense of ambition or motivation, and this can force them into a more focused state. This would be like lifting from your back instead of from your legs when lifting a weight. It temporarily brings around an improvement in your ability, but in the long term, it's something you want to avoid because it's not good for your health. We need to ensure we're meditating without strain.

The first thing to look at is our posture. If you're in this state of focus through tension, you'll often find your head is lowered, and your shoulders turn to curve in. You tend to fold in on yourself. Make sure your shoulders are back and your head is upright. Ensure your body is completely relaxed and you are not tense. Some people tense the back of their neck when they use this type of focus. The second thing to look at is your breathing. When we move into this emergency focus, we tend to use very shallow breathing. You can see this in someone playing a computer game when it's at a critical stage. You can see this when people are doing fine-tuned manual work when they have to do something challenging. Sometimes they do shallow breaths and even hold their breath.

CHAPTER 8: HOW TO MEDITATE

Our meditation should be accompanied by a beautiful, smooth, long breath from the abdomen and not from the chest. If we are relaxed and have deep regular breaths, then our mind will follow, and we can be sure we are focusing with the whole of our awareness, not just condensing all our energy on one point.

The next possible cause is a positive thing—that it's part of our adaptation. When we learn to meditate, we will start to free up energy that was constrained by unnecessary old habits or areas of functioning that weren't ideal. Meditation will lead to a higher current of energy going through your being. This increased heat can be considered like how impurities are removed—by increased temperature. You can think of it in terms of released energy from things that aren't needed any more. If this is the case, then this heat is to be embraced. You can dress in light clothing when practising meditation. You can be in a well-aired environment and think of this heat as light shining out like the sun shines forth goodness – you're shining positivity into the world. By viewing it this way, you'll find it as something to be embraced and enjoyed rather than something to be worried about. Maybe you can think about how the heat warms all your joints and organs and how this healthy increase of temperature focuses the mind. I've talked to Zen monks in the mountains who said that when they practice their meditation for a certain period of time every day, they don't need bed covers, but when they do less meditation and slack, they have to bring the bed covers back out.

I would recommend anyone who experiences this to study the myth of the phoenix and consider this process in their daily life. Whatever comes at you in life, transform it into something positive. Any thoughts that you have that aren't that useful, transform them. Roses grow best in animal waste. The lotus flower thrives in the mud. You can transform the worst aspects of your life into something more positive. By embracing this process in life, you will find it changes the feel of the process in your meditation.

2. Why do spontaneous movements occur during meditation practice?

This is something that starts to occur when people begin to deepen their meditation practice. These movements tend to be rhythmic, and they manifest as either a desire to move in a certain way or as a spontaneous, uncontrollable movement. Often, you'll see rocking. Sometimes it'll be a swaying movement. The most common you'll see will be a spiralling or circling type of expression. For some people, these can be quite strong, and there can even be a shaking movement to it. This is a manifestation of the evolution taking place. It's a way that our system is learning to adapt to our new levels of concentration and high levels of energy running through us. It is part of the clearing of barriers and blockages that need to take place for us to move to the next level.

Many meditation schools teach you to simply suppress these movements. They don't want you to get used to manifesting a different state of mind and a different way of being in your practice. I believe that these movements are a blessing, as they're calling on you to express a specific vibration or rhythm. To do this, I'm going to advise two methods. The first one is to find a way in your normal life to express the rhythm. It may be that you might like to practice a form of flowing yoga that moves from one posture to another with a similar kind of beat and type of motions. Maybe those circles would be manifested well in Tai Chi or Qi Gong. Perhaps it's time to learn to dance or use straightforward types of exercise like running or swimming, but to that manifested beat and rhythm. Typically, if you start to do this, your meditation will become still inside and out.

Another method you may like to use that is natural and beautiful, and I believe what these movements are calling for you to do, is to time your breath to the movement. To do this, you may keep your eyes slightly open so you have a sense of solidity and stability. Then, if your movements start to occur or the urge to move in a certain way happens, time your breathing with slightly more force than you usually would in meditation to the exact rhythm. You may need to slightly deepen and elongate the breath to form that rhythm, and as you do you, you find the movements naturally stop. Your new practice is to keep this breath to the same rhythm and feel like the movement that was coming forth. By doing this, you aid the purification process. You help the internal adaption to the new way of doing things, and this will allow you to evolve rather than put off that evolution.

3. Overcoming agitation and worry during meditation practice

This is an occurrence that sometimes happens during your meditation practice. This would be a period where whenever you sit down to perform your meditation, your mind drifts off to everyday matters. This tends to occur during times of change or worry. I'm not talking about the odd thought that has to do with mundane matters. I'm talking about a sense of agitation where your mind wants to be mulling things over, and the harder you fight against this, the worse it gets. When this occurs, there can be two causes for it. Rather than just trying to suppress the problem, I'm going to give some practical methods that will allow you to listen to what your mind is telling you and benefit from the situation.

The first circumstance is a time when your mind is trying to help you process or come to terms with what's happening. When there's a time of challenge or significant change, we all find times to plan and to adapt to those events. Some people like to do this internally and quietly, so they'll find some activity that allows them to mull things over gently. It could be gardening, or it could even be a television program or something that gives you enough preoccupation that you can still go back to the subject now and again. Other people tend to express themselves through words. They find people to talk things over with. So, the first thing to do is to make sure your mind has an opportunity to do what it needs to do for you. When you're settling down into meditation, it believes this is an excellent opportunity to help, so you need to give it better opportunities. Make sure you're sleeping enough; thus, your dreams and healing processes during your sleep are kicking in and working to their optimum. Make sure you have people to talk to if you enjoy talking things over, or make sure you have space in your life to process.

The other cause may be to do with the borderlines in your life. So rather than being a response to a period of business or a period of change, it's merely that you don't have separate sections to your life, and this means that it's hard for your deeper thinking

CHAPTER 8: HOW TO MEDITATE

processes to know when it should be thinking about what. We all know people who have problems with borderlines, so they are not fully engaging with what they're doing. When they are at work, they find ways to avoid work and to play in some way. But, because of this, in their spare time, they let work seep into that time so they can't fully engage with their family or the enjoyable activities they want to take part in. Practising clear borderlines in your undertakings and the different roles you have in life is a useful discipline. It strengthens the memory and allows you to learn and evolve in that role so that you can move to the next step and continue improving. By keeping these clear borderlines, you'll find that in your meditation, you'll have far less disturbance from other areas of life.

We all have unique ways of telling ourselves when it's time to do something else. For work, many people go to a different place. They wear different things. For their family life, they may even use different names for different situations. It may be that you're Mr. Jones when you're at work, but you're David when you're at home. Ever since meditation developed as an art, we have developed ways to tell our mind to switch gears. This could be a bell that rings at the beginning of the meditation session or two blocks being hit together. Some people like to wear different clothes, sit in a specific place in a particular position at a certain time, use specific beads for meditation, or light incense or a candle. Make sure you're fully utilizing these non-verbal messages. Whether you start to put on a certain type of music or burn a particular incense, these practices help create the atmosphere for the ideal meditation and tell your subconscious it's time to meditate.

MEDITATION TOOLS

CHAPTER 9

Meditation Tools: Why Do We Use Them?

Meditation tools are used to keep our minds present not only on the goals we wish to achieve but primarily as tools to help keep our focus on the present moment. Often when we do things habitually, they become so automatic we often perform an exercise without full awareness of what we are doing. Using these tools aid our attention and focus throughout meditation practice.

A List of Tools that May be Useful in Meditation Practice:

- A cushion
- Mala or prayer beads
- Bracelet
- A timer
- Incense
- Isis band

A Cushion

When starting, it is good to use a cushion to allow comfort during meditation. This enables the hips to keep their alignment until they open up more and to let the knees to sink. Often when we start meditating, our hips are restricted, so placing a cushion under us prevents discomfort or injury from misalignment.

How to Use Mala or Rosary Prayer Beads in Meditation

Mala and prayer beads have been used as a means of timing meditation practice in both Western and Eastern esoteric traditions for centuries. Their use is twofold. Firstly, their purpose is to keep the mind focused on the moment. Secondly, by wearing them, they act as a reminder of our goals to achieve enlightenment. As we use them, they develop a charge, which also aids in our practice. Such beads could be in the form of mala beads that the Indian yogis use, which also have knots in between that allows you to use specific methods of moving the beads through your hands. For a standard set of beads, some people tie knots in a piece of string.

To use beads as a time your Hermetic meditation you need to synchronise their movement to your breath. Before you begin, remind yourself of this goal. Take a few moments to reflect on what you are about to do and make sure your position is stable. Adjust it and take a few moments to let your breathing to settle down. Remind yourself that you are going to enter into a state of pure tranquillity, awareness, and complete connectedness. Allow yourself to relax. In your mind, this is a template for what your typical daily consciousness should be like. If you need to set a timer to monitor the length of time spent, now is the time to get your apparatus ready.

Now the aim is to invite in relaxation, natural awareness, and to clear the mind of all other thoughts. Take off your beads if you are wearing them, place them in your hand, and bring your attention to the breath.

There are lots of different ways you can hold your beads. I like to put them between my thumb and first finger. As you breathe in, move your thumb over the top of the bead. Then breathe out. Time your in and out breath with the movement of the bead and with your thumb. Imagine it as being precious. Allow yourself to fully relax and just watch it for a few moments.

This may sound challenging, but you know you can do it for one bead, so just focus on each bead at a time. Now, this exercise aims to use the mala beads as a tool to achieve a state of total tranquillity and awareness. If any thought or thing could distract you, let that flow past. After you finish your exercise, put on the beads to wear during the day. Notice how your breathing is more relaxed. In your regular life, take this exercise with you. Wear your beads and let the new vibrations and state of consciousness acquired from this exercise be present with you throughout the day. Most people will find one whole mala of 108 beads takes about ten minutes.

Bracelet

Just like wearing your meditation beads, a bracelet can be a great visual reminder to prompt you to practice or to achieve the goal you set yourself. For example, if you are working on awareness throughout the day, wearing the bracelet as a visual reminder keeps us focused and not forget the intended goal we set for ourselves.

CHAPTER 9: MEDITATION TOOLS

Stop Watch

A stop watch is an excellent way to time your meditation and regulate your practice. It's also a unique way to test your progress. When performing mediation, it's useful to time how long you can maintain this state of consciousness. Record the number of disturbances in a given time. For example, you may start with five minutes and build up to twenty minutes. The use of the timer allows you to measure the goal clearly, and you can observe and record your progress.

Incense

Incense has great significance within spiritual traditions and is reputed for purifying the surroundings and bringing forth an assembly of buddhas, bodhisattvas, and gods. This practice is still very much in proliferation across Asia amongst Buddhist and Taoist traditions. When you enter a temple, it is customary to offer a lighted incense stick to each of the deities as an acknowledgement and sign of respect. In the Western tradition and ancient Egypt, this was no different. It was the custom to light incense as a sign of respect to the gods and would be perceived as an insult if not performed. Moses was instructed by God to construct an altar to burn incense in honour of God's glory. This remains a practice that continues in many religions of Abrahamic origins.

Our sense of smell has a very powerful effect on the mind. Many people find that the act of lighting incense helps get them into the correct state for relaxed focus and meditation. Perhaps this is why the use of incense has been so universal in different traditions. Not only is it a symbolic offering to the heavens or purification of the space, but also a powerful trigger for a heightened state of awareness.

Isis Band

In ancient times, meditation practice would take place in a specially designed room in the temple or house of life. This practice was started by the ancient Egyptians and continued in the healing temples of the Greeks. A darkened room would be painted jet black and scented with incense for concentrated practice.

In later times when such temples were rare, the practitioners used a different method to aid their practice that would bring around a similar focus and sensory deprivation as in the temple. The band of Isis was a thin strip of black material gathered from the clothes used to dress a sacred statue of Isis or another deity in the temple. This band was anointed with holy scented oils and had symbols representing the Great Good.

The band was used rather like the stole of modern Christianity or the kesa of Buddhism. It was worn during any spiritual activity to signify to the wearer the importance of his undertaking. The band represents all that is good and the divine order. The Virgin Isis that brought everything to light. When worn, it would remind the practitioner to tune into goodness and do everything with the best of intentions during meditation. The band was worn over the eyes like a blindfold. This would, to some degree, be akin to the darkened room of the temple.

The band on the simplest level represented love and was also used to link things together during spells of binding or unification. During these exercises, the band was worn on a specific arm or body part to bring about healing or a form of charge.

RITUAL DISCIPLINES OF MEDITATION

CHAPTER 10

Now I would like to discuss the ritual disciplines of meditation. These are the techniques that allow us to move from one state to another. It is an area that is often neglected. Most schools focus on environmental things, such as what you wear, where you sit, and how your body is positioned.

These transitional techniques are fundamental because without them, people can find it hard to move from their ordinary waking consciousness to a very focused state that is needed for meditation training. It is very hard to spend ten minutes working on one subject, like a breathing or energy exercise, then switch to being extremely focused on another exercise. Following are instructions for how to clear your mind of all thoughts with a clear transition that clearly states what you are stopping doing and what you are starting.

When you first sit down to do your routine, the actual gesture of taking off the beads is something that clearly states you are about to practice. Likewise, many environmental factors could suggest to your mind, like what you are wearing, where you are sitting, and lighting incense to inform you that this is practice time. If you find yourself in a situation where these external symbols don't always exist, a specific gesture can be the clear marker of transition. Use your intuition for determining your gestures, such as a visualisation or perhaps an affirmation or prayer. To visualise yourself in the perfect state for meditation, you could offer a prayer for help. Some people have a special spiritual name that communicates to your entire being that it is time to practice.

The next thing you want to do is some form of specific protection exercise to clear all negative influences and to take control of our practice.

A spoken Intention

Now let us say what our meditation is going to be. Clear you mind for a moment and then focus on the clear intention. Hold your beads as in the image below:

Figure ix: Holding the beads

Take a moment to visualize exactly what you are about to do. Use a specific phrase or statement of intent. 'I am going to clear my mind of all thoughts. "I will watch my breath for ten minutes" or "I will become at one with all that is good in the world". These are examples of course this statement would vary depending on the meditation you are about to undertake.

'Visualize success, and then it is time for your meditation.'

Once you have completed your meditation, it is time to move to the next exercise. We now need to make sure that the original intention is completely gone. We use the following posture, which is called 'closing the door.' You open your arms out palms facing upwards, raise them above your head, then bring the arms down and palms facing downwards. Please view the image below. You can feel that intention as you do this exercise. It is particularly important when we have been doing something that involves visualisation and clear that intention, visualisation, mantra, or energy away. Even if you believe that your original intention is banished, this is still an important discipline as it helps us indicate a distinguished end.

Figure x: 'Closing the door' posture.

When it is time for your next meditation, once again, hold the beads in the same position. If, for example, your contemplation is on fire, we imagine success in this and say, 'I am about to think about fire for ten minutes to enter into the mysteries of fire and to contemplate it fully without disturbance for ten minutes.'

When it is time for our next meditation, we once again use the action of 'closing the door.' You can imagine how important it is when it comes to energy exercises. Then at the end of the exercise, we need a gesture that states to yourself it is over and return your focus to the normal state of consciousness.

Start with putting your beads back to where you usually keep them. Imagine that you are absorbing the lessons from the higher state of consciousness with your gesture. Imagine that visualisation disperses now. We are moving back to everyday life, taking the lessons with us. These disciplines are crucial as they allow us to have purity in each exercise. I have met people who have been practicing for many years and part of the problem has been that one exercise is causing a problem with another. Moving from one to another is a foundational skill that becomes increasingly important as we work in more advanced energetic ways, so make sure you are fastidious in practicing this.

The Most Powerful Rituals of The Greatest Adepts

An interesting question I have often received is, 'What are the most powerful rituals practiced by the greatest adepts?' This question is very important, and the answer has great significance and may surprise some people.

The Hermetic adept has gone beyond having a magical practice and has fully embraced magical life. For them, the mystical and mundane have truly joined as one. If we were to follow the life of the adept practitioner, we would see that he or she would instead put more into every action or event in life than most people. Upon waking, a powerful intention is sent out into the world that ripples and influences success and positive outcomes throughout the day. Upon getting up and showering, that shower becomes a powerful banishing ritual. As the water runs, it washes away all negative influences. When getting dressed, remember each item of clothing in ritual practice, and other spiritual disciplines have a special significance and power. When eating, be a true eucharist with the food bringing great blessings and hidden transformations. During the day, we would see that everyday actions are completed consciously and that the adept fully employs all their magical knowledge and skill. When the key is inserted into the lock and the front door is locked, a barrier is put around the house, keeping it free from negative influences.

During the day, every word is a word of power constructed using Hermetic principles and filled with might. Everyday gestures are magical gestures. Kindness imparted in a smile. A blessing in a kiss on the cheek. Healing in a handshake. Before the Hermetic adept, objects take on a hidden, powerful significance. A wallet not only holds money but attracts money to be inside it. A car is not only a physical vehicle but also takes the practitioner precisely to where he or she wishes to go. The practitioner will use all their senses so that they can detect what is happening on multiple levels when they talk to someone, go to a new environment, or hold an object. By fully understanding the principles of sympathy, the adept practitioner can attract the right characters, influences, and persons at any given situation and allow them to depart when their influence is no longer favourable.

In this sense, the Hermetic practitioner lives their entire life improving their skills and advancing in every moment. Even sleep becomes a doorway to exploring higher realms of consciousness and improving oneself. These are the most powerful rituals practiced by the greatest adepts.

HOW TO STICK TO A MEDITATION ROUTINE

CHAPTER 11

The most commonly asked questions I receive are, 'Do you have any advice on sticking to a meditation regime?' and 'How would you discipline yourself to stick to a meditation routine?'

When contemplating meditation, the word 'routine' is the key point. People are creatures of habit, so there are probably things in your daily routine that you do with ease, for example, getting up, cleaning your teeth, having a bath, etc. Since these chores have become a part of your daily routine and are necessary, they present very little resistance. You barely think about them. We can apply the same method with your meditation practice to include and make it part of that routine. It is best to have a set location that is convenient and as quiet as possible. Maybe it has the accoutrements associated with meditation that you use. Maybe use a specific cushion, or burn incense and practice in that place as often as possible. It is also powerful to practice at a set time every day. Maybe at seven o'clock in the morning and seven o'clock in the evening. Then that becomes your meditation time from then on. As your mind and subconscious get used to this routine, you will find that some of the barriers that get in your way start to disappear. It also helps you to discipline yourself and to cut things out of your life to allow you to stick to the routine.

A lot of people complain they do not have enough time. But if you look at their life, they spend hours every evening watching television or socializing, and it is a question of what they would rather do, which brings me to the next point, which is attitude. A lot of people talk about the difficulty of meditation. This may be due to the fact they are viewing meditation as some form of negative and challenging exercise. Perhaps they feel that it is something they need to make themselves do, rather than seeing it as a wonderful and beautiful thing. To even have the opportunity is magnificent. When we view meditation correctly, it becomes a daily joy, as it is a chance to bring yourself into balance, harmony, to relax, to develop your mind, and find out more about who you are and the world around you. When seen through this lens, meditation becomes something you look forward to, rather than trying to make yourself stick to it. Every day you are motivated to practice because of the benefits that are felt.

Another aspect regarding the attitude towards meditation is that I have noticed the way people view meditation can aid or hinder them with their practice. Knowing this enables us to be in a powerful position to see this as a practice that will help us and to discipline ourselves, with the correct attitude for achieving success in that practice. There are various methods people use to motivate themselves:

1. To view it as a challenge. They look forward to that challenge, and when they are practising, they try their best not to allow themselves to become lazy or absent-minded in their practice. Some people would find that stressful, and that approach would be viewed as unfavourable for them.

2. Other people view it as a sacred duty, like praying or doing good works. They are not doing it for themselves but for other people, because they want to have a better effect on the world and ensure they are a better person to do that.

3. Other people see it as a necessity. They get themselves into a mental position that it is like sleeping or eating—one must do it. Whatever situation puts you in a position of strength is the one you should cultivate.

I would like to discuss the obstacles you may face and how to use them to your advantage. In this case, use every distraction and turn it to your advantage. This is a powerful principle and practice that, once understood, can be used to gain ability in all skills in life. Thus, use every distraction and reason not to practice to your advantage. You may find one of the little tricks your mind plays on you. Perhaps you will convince yourself of a legitimate reason why tonight or this morning is not an appropriate time to practice. Your mind will say tomorrow is when the new regime starts. When tomorrow comes, thirty years may have passed, and still, the new regime never appeared. Whenever you start getting the feeling that you will begin tomorrow, it means it is time to do it NOW. That feeling is reminding you to grasp the moment because procrastination means that you never get to live the life you want to live or do what you want to do.

Another common challenge is the excuses or reasons why it was not possible to meditate at the allotted time. Often not having enough time is the common factor. It could be to do with being busy or being in the company of others or only not having the meditation area to practice. Whatever that is, you need to make that part of the challenge to improve your routine.

Let us imagine you have been traveling all day or have had a social event, and you missed your normal time. You get back and think you are too tired. Well, that is brilliant!

CHAPTER 11: HOW TO STICK TO A MEDITATION ROUTINE

The challenge that evening is to meditate and remain calm, clear, and focused when extremely tired. Make the negative part of the positive. Like weightlifting, you make the adversity part of the training. The same is if you have a sore back. Lay down to meditate. The challenge is to meditate around that injury or around that pain.

A great master once said to me, 'It is good sometimes to have something to ignore.' Incorporate that into whatever it is that starts to prevent you from your routine. You will find your mind comes up with all sorts of tricks, saying there is a good reason why you can't stick to your discipline tonight. Turn those reasons into the reasons to stick to it. Then you have understood one of the fundamentals of self-mastery. These are the principals that I have learned to stick to a meditation regime, and they can be applied to all disciplines. I hope they help you in your practice.

Furthermore, there are three essential tools you can use that are extremely powerful. They are a visual reminder, the inclusion of a new routine added with an existing one, and the power of using a vow. I believe that you will be convinced of their effectiveness once you have deployed them in your life. For me, using these tools has been the most effective means of bringing around awareness.

Methods to Establish a Meditation Routine

1. A Visual Reminder

   This can be something that provides a cue for action. That could be a bracelet, mala beads, an icon, or perhaps a particular colour that is meaningful to you or symbolic of your goal. It could even be an object. It is also something that no one else has contact with. All these things are incredibly effective and something you can enforce with your imagination. To have a physical reminder works almost like a charge that holds the memory for you to access when needed.

2. Add a New Routine onto an Existing One

   Introduce a new routine and integrate it with one that is already established. For example, you get up, brush your teeth, take a shower, then take your beads from the side of the bed, and when you put them on, this then becomes an indication that you are ready to perform your practice. You may add this order onto an existing routine so that the mind does not resist and accepts this as part of the new routine. After showering, you sit down, do your practice, then make breakfast, etc. Then your meditation practice seamlessly fits into your already established routine.

3. The Power of a Vow

I have found this method one of the most potent ways to aid with adhering to a discipline. I use this method for extremely strenuous disciplines. Usually, I use this method if something is challenging, or I need the motivation to do it every day, especially if they are necessary but tedious.

The way to do this is to have a very specific vow. For example, I will perform this meditation twice a day for one hundred and eight days. The way to do this is to use a physical object like a necklace or bracelet to represent this vow, so it is not forgotten. Then use a dramatic and intriguing way to record your successes. Perhaps use one hundred and eight incense sticks so that every day as you do your meditation, you burn one. Or maybe you use a bucket full of stones, and every day when you have finished your martial arts or physical exercises, you take one of those stones and throw it in the river until the bucket is empty.

I have seen people tick dates off a calendar or create a recurring task on their google tasks list, so it counts down the number of times. Or even make an appointment in their diary that recurs until that day runs out. For me, the more visual the measuring system, the more motivational it is. Maybe you could scratch or mark each bead on a one hundred and eight beads mala necklace. Or perhaps you could have a set number of beads on your wrist and every day you take one off. All these methods inform the mind that you are succeeding daily and assist in building momentum.

Taking a vow like this creates a very powerful message to yourself. Having a visual aid conveys that this is going to happen no matter what. This helps the subconscious to perform the task without resistance and keeps the task interesting. It is motivating to be able to see the incense sticks disappearing. Or to see the bucket emptying as you toss the stones. That is my number one tip in sticking to something difficult to do. Taking a vow and making a visual symbolic fulfilment of that vow is a satisfying thing and ensures the accomplishment of the goal.

4. Using Appointments to Aid with Keeping to a Meditation Practice

Here is another excellent tip that will help you stick to a meditation routine. It is particularly suitable for busy people and for business people who work with a diary a lot. Use your blackberry, smartphone, or iPad and book a reoccurring appointment with yourself for when you want to do your meditation every day. Make sure you choose the most dramatic form of reminder. Maybe a text message option or an email. Sometimes a beep or a sound will be enough. This way, you are working with an established discipline. The fact you are used to sticking to appointments, this appointment system will help you work with the way you already operate. Since it is in the diary, you will not tend to use the time elsewhere if someone wants you to do something else. This is very powerful for business people and a way of telling your subconscious that this is something that is going to happen every day. This trick can be used for any form of discipline, whether it be physical exercise or study. You do not have to only use it for meditation. The combination of using all three techniques creates a powerful combination.

Learning from Distractions that Occur During Meditation Practice

When you have practiced meditation for some time and mastered the art to some degree, you will find your mind naturally starts to still. When our mind stills and our thoughts slow down, we can watch our mind. Often in daily life, we don't take time to listen to our inner selves. If negative emotions come up from the past, we push them down and get on with our day. We do our best to avoid rather than deal with problems. Perhaps our intuition has been trying to warn us about something for several months, and we have done all we can to quiet that down. When someone is upset and ignored or cut out, they often start to shout.

Whenever our mind is distracted or cannot relax, we can look at the cause of the distraction and learn about ourselves. When you have managed to overcome the lie or sit still and concentrate on your breathing with some ease, then you can start on this stage. In this stage, you are advised to make a note of your distractions. These distractions will probably come in one of the following forms.

Fear and Worries

Painful emotional responses to past events that have not been dealt with. Fearful thoughts about the future, including:

- Wishes and coveting thoughts about the future
- Fantasies and exciting thoughts
- Repeating past events
- You will also have some disturbances that tend not to repeat themselves, such as jealous thoughts or excitement about mundane life
- Mundane worries about everyday events
- Repetition of things you have seen or read in the day

Whenever you notice a repeated disturbance, take a note of it after your meditation. Some people like to categorise it under one of the above headings. For the time being, don't make any effort to think about the disturbance. It is part of the process of learning to relax with these thoughts no matter what they are. Just simply make a note of the disturbance. If you find yourself naturally thinking about the subject matter during daily life, then let yourself do so.

During this time, you should work your daily meditation up to about twenty minutes both morning and night. You will find that in the time that this process follows many of the disturbances that you noted will simply disappear. They will slowly and naturally decrease their appearances without even knowing meditation resolves their causes. While you go about your daily business, your unconscious mind and higher aspect of yourself are dealing with the causes of these disturbances. Additionally, many of the mental blocks and neurosis in humans are illusionary. That is to say that it is the fear of them that makes then persist.

When you learn to relax and treat the thoughts and subject matter with calm detachment, they disappear like shadows when illuminated. At the end of the three months, you will notice that your disturbances tend to be few and far between. You will feel that they are almost coming from a distant place and will experience periods of calmness between thoughts. You may still get the day to day thoughts but will find that your persistent disturbances are based around a few base subjects. This stage typically takes two to five months.

Is Meditation Selfish?

Sometimes people question the value of meditation and a path of self-development. It is sometimes asked whether one should be assisting others in a practical way rather than spending time pursuing this form of activity since there is an idea of perceived selfishness. Sometimes this question is asked but from the other point of view. Sometimes those who practice daily meditation find their compassion and awareness increasing, and they feel they want to assist the world, and there is nothing they can do that is enough.

The answer in both cases is the same. In reality, we do not practice meditation disciplines for ourselves. As we continue to improve ourselves, the positive effect on our surroundings is also noted. In reality, we are assisting others for the greater good of the ALL. An example of this, we know how one person drives their car can have a considerable effect on the other drivers on the road. One's journey can be significantly affected depending on this. Just think how one person can change the mood of the whole situation depending on their behaviour. It is possible to see the results of these kinds of effects over an entire lifetime.

So when we raise our consciousness, improve our clarity and vision, and cultivate virtue in ourselves, we thus having a positive effect on the human race in general. Just like every cell in our body has an essential purpose, so does your life. We were born in charge of ourselves, so that is where our number one focus should be. We were given this mind, and this body let us use them to the highest ability.

In conclusion, yes, we should do good works, and these should be a natural reflection of our nature. On our path, we create a paradise within ourselves, so we are aiming to think the thoughts we would like to think. We are aiming to do the things we would like to see happening in the world. Say the things we would like to hear people saying. We want to be a living testament to our standards and to let that spread from ourselves.

SECTION 2

INVITING THE GREAT GOOD INTO DAILY LIFE

FORMING A REGULAR AND BALANCED LIFE

CHAPTER 12

One of the most important goals, when we choose to follow a spiritual path or a form of meditation practice for self-improvement, is to develop and establish a balanced life. As we start to exert an effort to establish a routine, life will challenge our qualities, character, and priorities at each step. If you do not prioritize a balanced lifestyle from the onset, you will find it is a bit like trying to build a castle on sand. We have to keep readjusting the foundation as we continue.

A balanced lifestyle consists of having:

1. Clear priorities
2. A social network of positive people
3. Harmonious interaction with the world
4. Emotional balance
5. Material affairs completely in order

When trying to harmonise your life, you may find that there are aspects of your personality that challenge you during this process. If this happens, understand that this is part of your spiritual progress and growth. These are the very aspects of your personality which you need to balance and harmonise to further develop.

An important thing to consider is the redirection of goals. For instance, you might find that instead of practising meditation, you release that intent by talking about it, watching videos, and exerting energy to do anything but the actual practice. Sometimes I meet people who research and read copious amounts of literature, but their life is void of practice. This is another form of displacement activity.

Discern your intentions when following a spiritual routine. Firstly, consider your spiritual practice as your primary goal in life. Secondly, dedication to that practice is at the top of your priorities. By organizing your life this way, your consistent practice will allow you to achieve balance in all other areas of life. By making it a priority, it operates like a blessing to the rest of our life in every way.

The next area of life that we wish to address is our social life. This refers to creating harmony with others as far as possible. We want to attract and cultivate friendships that are positive and support our goals. If we must interact with people contrary to our goals, then we can see them as training aids, by not only learning from their errors but also viewing them as training partners. In this way, their attacks or disturbances can instead be considered as a training exercise for us to practice our new, balanced way of doing things. If there are any ongoing, unsolved dramatics in your life, it is time to solve them now so you may cultivate a harmonious existence.

Recovery is a crucial thing, and to do this well, time management is the key. Make sure you develop regular sleeping habits and have enough spare time to recover. The ability to rest and recover is something that sincerely reaps benefits now and later on in this path. If you find yourself thinking you don't have enough time to recover, then examine how you choose to spend your time. Do you sit in front of the TV flicking through channels for hours? If so, make recovery the priority. Or maybe you feel too overworked to get enough rest? If this is the case, then you would be surprised by how much your stamina, concentration, and ability will improve by sorting out your recovery. There are direct correlations between your mental abilities and whether you are sleeping correctly and regularly. So, it may seem like you are sacrificing work time, but in the long-term, it will easily pay off.

There are other areas of our lives which are vital for us to keep balanced. We often neglect our emotional needs, so ensure you receive inspirational stimulation such as going to beautiful places and doing things you enjoy. If you find yourself in a particular rut, then try going for a walk or into a garden every day. Connecting to the natural world has been proven to help alleviate stress. Make sure that you eat a balanced diet and exercise regularly to not only keep your body working well but also to cultivate a balanced mental state.

As far as your material affairs are concerned, it is important to set your life up so that you can pay for things in the material world, all matters are in order, and your outside interaction with the world reflects what you want to achieve inside. So make your surroundings beautiful, harmonious, and in order. This helps to prevent material difficulties from unduly interfering with the more important parts of your life.

To truly progress, whether in meditation or daily life, we need a balanced platform from which we can work from. This includes developing a regulated and structured life. Establish routines that support all your desired goals. Depending on your personality, you may find you have many goals or perhaps not many at all. If you fall into the former category, determine what is important to you, since having too many goals at once can be counterproductive. If you are unable to limit your goals, choose ones to focus on at this moment in life and write the others down to be completed at a later stage. If you have a vague idea of the direction you are going in but no set goal, this action can bring clarity. Creating a clear schedule of your allotted tasks prevents you from feeling overwhelmed, allows you to prioritise, and ensures that you have an honest, congruent, clear vision of what you are trying to accomplish. Sometimes just putting what you want into words is enough to banish any inner conflict and counterproductive behaviour.

A method I have found useful is to make personal appointments for the activities that are important to me, such as meditation or activity related to one of my goals. Scheduling these as daily tasks means they are not forgotten during the day and also helps me steadily work towards the goal. Interestingly, when we are dealing with our personality, we may find one area tends to be more prominent. Mistakenly, this area could then become the sole focus of our goal and take precedence over all things in our life. For example, we may decide that our main wish is to become sincerely and genuinely respected, be a good friend to others, bring abundance into our life, or cultivate good health. These are all noble goals, but when one of these goals becomes too dominant, we can become imbalanced and confused. Rather than having a wish for genuine respect and a noble life, we could have the urge for fame at any cost. Instead of cultivating genuine positive allies, we focus on popularity. Instead of wishing for abundance, we wish to be obscenely wealthy. Our attention to exercise and diet is to accentuate our physical appearance and fitness rather than genuine and total health. We should wish to achieve our goals through balance and not by becoming obsessed with a particular area in our life. By using an appointment system, we can ensure our time and effort is allocated in a balanced way.

Another consideration we should make is our interaction with others. If our interactions are lacking harmony, we may need to seek out the imbalances which are causing it. If you find yourself seeking a very strong emotional stimulus, it is usually a sign that you are not recovering fully. Tiredness often dulls our emotional awareness, causing us to seek out stronger stimuli to override our senses. Additionally, a deficiency in personal energy can expose us to poor decisions regarding our choice of words, which can then lead to misunderstandings and stir further emotional responses. At times of tiredness and high stress, we need to move our focus from lofty goals and big achievements to creating a wholesome sense of contentment and harmony in our everyday lives. Then later on, we can start thinking about creating excellence in other areas in a balanced way. This is paramount if we want success in all aspects of our practice and life. You will find there is a direct relationship between creating a balanced and harmonious lifestyle and your imperturbability in daily life.

Another consideration we should make is our interaction with others. If our interactions are lacking harmony, we may need to seek out the imbalances which are causing it. If you find yourself seeking a very strong emotional stimulus, it is usually a sign that you are not recovering fully. Tiredness often dulls our emotional awareness, causing us to seek out stronger stimuli to override our senses. Additionally, a deficiency in personal energy can expose us to poor decisions regarding our choice of words, which can then lead to misunderstandings and stir further emotional responses. At times of tiredness and high stress, we need to move our focus from lofty goals and big achievements to creating a wholesome sense of contentment and harmony in our everyday lives. Then later on, we can start thinking about creating excellence in other areas in a balanced way. This is paramount if we want success in all aspects of our practice and life. You will find there is a direct relationship between creating a balanced and harmonious lifestyle and your imperturbability in daily life.

THE EYE OF THE HORUS—BEING IN EVERY MOMENT

CHAPTER 13

Those who have been undertaking Hermetic Meditation for some time will notice certain improvements in their consciousness. They describe feeling more aware in daily life, more able to focus on things, and the ability to complete them with calmness and efficiency. Some students even note that others around them have noticed how much they have changed. At this point we want to amplify this effect and stabilise this higher level of functioning. The following exercise may be simple, but it is a very powerful method, so get ready for a big change in how you interact with the world, your sense of self, and how other people view you.

Think back to school and the group of children who seemed to be playing football every lunchtime. Despite practising day after day, year after year, they never seemed to really improve in proportion. It seems unbelievable doesn't it? Imagine practicing a skill an hour a day for ten years; I would expect my skill level to be very good indeed, no matter how hard the skill.

This situation, no matter how strange sounding, is the norm. Have you ever noticed how many things people do without really trying? They may ask directions, but then don't make any effort to memorise the directions they are given. Perhaps you have noticed some people who constantly lose the same objects or make the same mistakes with no sign of learning. Everyone has a friend that complains about the same problem but makes no effort to change what they are doing in the situation and constantly deploy the same strategy. So why aren't we improving upon the things we get to practise again and again?

The truth is unless we make an effort to improve our abilities, any one task will remain the same. We have a tendency to progress to the level that is required to avoid discomfort and then stay at that point. Only when we do something with the intent to learn, with an effort to do our best, will improvement be our result.

Please take a moment to imagine what your life would be like if from this moment on you fully engaged with all tasks. Picture what would happen if you really tried to improve every undertaking you are a part of. Every day you would improve on all levels, with unbelievable results. Visualise what would happen if whenever you needed to use your memory in a task, no matter how mundane, you made a real effort. Just think of the knock-on effect in other areas of your life, how your memory would begin to improve on a daily basis, and what long term effects this could really have. Now imagine this across all areas of your life. What if every time you communicated with someone you really tried your best to communicate as effectively as possible? Using the right words, tone, timing and method to achieve the best possible outcome. This would lead to you being more efficient. Maybe instead of several emails going back and forth, the first would be enough? The extra time this would free up would allow you to put your focus into other areas, continually improving. Imagine if every time you wrote your signature you treated it like a calligraphy class, when you placed your glass on the table you did it with precision and care, or if every step you took was with full calm awareness. Soon every movement and action become a practice on balanced coordination and ability. From outside it would seem as though you are naturally talented at all sports, physical undertakings, or activity. Your mind and focus would become honed and perfected with every waking moment.

Take a few moments to imagine if this principle spread like a light throughout your whole being, covering all aspects of life. If when you rested you really took time to relax and recover, when you imagined you really pictured things, and when you made love you really did so with all your heart, fully engaging with every moment with the whole of your being.

Have you ever heard the saying, 'The whole is greater than the sum of its parts?' If so, you may be able to picture how each and every improvement can have a knock-on effect on everything else, resulting in improvements far greater than you may at first believe possible.

From this moment onwards make a silent vow to yourself that you will make the best effort towards every single thing you do. Don't put anything beyond you or beneath you. Every action you take will be done with full wakefulness and direction. You will know when you get to the exact state when a sense of wholesome joy forms. When you get dressed in the morning do it to the best of your ability. When you exercise, study, work, tidy, etc., really aim to improve. Apply this to all aspects of your life, from every mouthful you eat to every word or action. Once this is a habit, suddenly everything becomes easier.

This practice is a sunlamp on your soul and will speed your progress in Hermetics in a way few other things can. Really focus on the areas you have previously found hard but be aware that humans have various mechanisms to avoid things we find hard. We decide we are not that kind of person or look at some tasks with disdain. Sometimes a big change in attitude or sense of self is needed. Sometimes you need to let go of past events, opinions, and even overcome the doubts and prejudices of others. Errors are an important part of learning and should be embraced as such. Remember to apply your growing ability to be steadfast and imperturbable to your daily life and keep focused on your goal.

HOW TO DEAL WTH PERSISTENT DISTURBANCES

CHAPTER 14

This is a most crucial step in the process. As you fine tune your practise, you need to overcome the disturbances that continue to haunt you. The disturbances that do not leave at their own accord and tend to come from some distinct sources. They can be unfulfilled wishes, regrets from the past that you have not dealt with, parts of your animal self that you lack control of, of perhaps instincts or urges that are strong in you. Either way, now is the time to start to think about your disturbances for these are aspects of the self that are asking for help to join with the great good.

Contemplate their Sources

You will probably find that some of them come from the same base motivation. For example, though you may not have realised before, you may notice that you have disturbances that are all caused by a territorial instinct. Perhaps you have jealous thoughts about others and also covet other peoples' partners. You may find those seemingly unrelated disturbances come from the experience of a single event in your past. Perhaps that even has caused you both fear of change and self-hatred. Either way, now is the time to analyse the disturbances and their possible sources. Do not let anything remain uncovered because knowledge is power.

During this process, you must continue to remain calm to the disturbances if they continue to appear in your meditation sessions. For some students, this may be a challenge. They may find it hard to prevent themselves from thinking of some line of inquiry about a disturbance previously made during contemplation.

Now comes the time to calm and eliminate your disturbances. You should see this as your highest duty to evolve and transform yourself in this manner. Know that not only are you transforming and overcoming any mental glitches you may have acquired from your experiences in this world. You are also overcoming harmful and disruptive characteristics in yourself that, through your birthright or karmic debt, are part of your mental makeup. In addition to the previously mentioned, you will also learn to control many aspects of yourself that a normal human never does.

Each disturbance should be put through a fourfold scheme of treatment. Sometimes the disturbance will disappear before the end of the cycle. If this is so, then it is okay to continue and start on the next disturbance. Through this methodology, the practitioner will genuinely learn to turn base metals into gold.

Listening

First of all, listen to your disturbance. Think about what it is trying to tell you. Take time to try to understand what this message could be about. Is this a gentle nag over something that you need to do in your life. Don't glorify your shortcomings or faults. Too many people use spirituality as an excuse to be lazy or immoral. You should be able to lead a normal, responsible life. Without this, no magical development is possible. During this process, any imbalance in your life will become clear. For example, if you continue to worry about your financial position or your job, you should probably look to see what you are going to have to change to bring this area of your life into harmony. Listen to this message. The monkey is chattering about something, but what is making it nervous? What has made it wild? The animal part of your mind often can see danger before you! You wouldn't want to try to calm the monkey mind down only to find out that it was trying to warn you about an approaching snake! If you see the advice is right, then it's time to change your life. Make the changes and ignore this disturbance for a few months. It should disappear. However, if you look and see that there is no problem and that this disturbance is illogical, other methods are needed.

Expression

Our passions are like a burning fire inside our souls. Heat and pressure must be expressed. When your disturbance turns out not to be any form of advice, it may be an area of your personality or emotions that are vying to be expressed. For example, you may be mentally going over potential confrontations simply because you have never managed to express immense anger from a past event. Perhaps then you are creating situations that allow you to be angry in your imagination over either the event itself or another less related event or a potential scenario. Search to see the underlying emotion or urge that makes you stick to this disturbance.

Boring disturbances never stick and are easy to resist. Only emotive thought hangs around and captivates us. Think about what it is that you need to get out. Remember that the causes of disturbances are not always the obvious ones. For example, sometimes it can be an enjoyable emotion or past event that haunts you. Perhaps an event that you can't accept has passed or that you can no longer experience. Sometimes these disturbances are not about past issues either. They are areas of yourself that don't find expression in your life. Either way, you should put these emotions to good work. If your disturbance is about a past event., you should find a healthy way to make your feeling clear about this event. You must find your own way of expressing this emotion. Use your rational mind to choose. Perhaps you could inform people involved unless you are unable to contact them or it is dangerous to contact these people. Maybe it's time to express your disturbance to a friend or professional. If this is not an option, you must find another way of expressing the original emotion through some expressive means.

There is sure to be some method suited to the individuality of every reader, be it through art, music, words, or physical movement. If nothing else is available, the practitioner may use his imagination to rehearse a meeting with the situation again and imagine himself dealing with the situation as before. Then with each session, imagine the emotional response fading until the practitioner is quite sure that no emotion towards the event remains unexpressed. A similar exercise can be arranged where the practitioner imagines informing the persons involved or chastising, forgiving, forgetting, or ignoring those individuals. Whichever method the practitioner chooses, he must practice until he is quite sure that this even has no hold on him any more. Perhaps the disturbance is discovered to be an expression of an unexpressed aspect of the practitioner's personality. For example, if a practitioner imagined being able to seduce women, that perhaps was suitable before his falling in love. Then the practitioner would have to find a proper outlet of this urge. Be it through affection and wooing his love or through the sublimation of his urges into exercise or other pursuits. Whatever the element in the personality, the same rule applies. First, make your enemy work for you! It's your energy. Use it how you like. Once the emotion or urge is expressed, the disturbances should subside.

Acceptance

To accept something, you must learn to deal with the situation mentally. Many disturbances are about things that we find hard to accept or deal with. Sometimes this can be on a large scale, like an inability to accept that there is so much pain and destruction in the world, or that humans are capable of such terrible acts. Some disturbances of the mind are simply due to awe at the understandable, miraculous nature of existence and the unanswered questions in the world and life. You will find that everyone has their own way of dealing with things. Some of the most basic advice a layperson can give you is useful at this stage.

The six main methods of helping you accept and deal with disturbances are as follows:

Contemplation on Life

In this contemplation, you consider the subject of your disturbance and its relevance to your life. The aim is to see how much emotional importance this subject has to you in your existence. Think about how this subject affects your life and your enjoyment of life. Think about how much of your life is devoted to this subject matter. Think about how important this subject is to you. Go over past events and see how you have reacted to situations and events relevant to this disturbance. Think about how important you want this subject to be to you. Try to get the subject categorised clearly. Imagine what difference it would make for you if this subject were of no importance to you.

Contemplation on Time

In this contemplation, you are to imagine the importance of the matter in the grand scheme of things. Start at your birth and think if all the disturbance mattered to you at this stage.

Review your life year by year to the best of your ability and see how much this problem impacted each period of your life. See how small that disturbance is in the grand scheme of life. Keep going until you reach the present day and see how much this affects you now. Continue year upon year into the future.

Imagine how much this will affect you if you simply let the disturbance carry on. Continue until the time of your death. Imagine your funeral and think about how much this disturbance affects you now. Imagine as your body disappears and becomes part of the earth. Look back over your lifetime and see how little importance the disturbance had in the grand scheme of your life. See how unworthy of your attention this disturbance is compared to what life has to offer. The practitioner should continue with this exercise until he is quite sure of the triviality of the disturbance in the grand scheme of time, and he feels deeply that this understanding has sunk to his heart. Practitioners with a great deal of imaginary power can, in subsequent occasions, imagine the effect of the disturbing subject matter from the dawn of time.

Contemplation on the Changing Nature of Existence

Think of your disturbance. Imagine how things change in the world. Start with imagining people that you know have changed. Imagine people you have known that have recovered and healed from illness. Perhaps you know someone who recovered from a long-term illness that people thought would be here forever. Imagine yourself when you are ill.

Think about how perhaps you felt like nothing would ever change and were worried that you would never get better. Think of the gardener mowing the grass or trimming a tree. Think about how plants change and grow. No matter what the gardener does, eventually they will change. They will overcome his best effort to keep things stable. Either they will outlive the gardener or they won't. Either way, the garden changes.

Contemplate All the Events in the World

Think of the change in animals and countries. Think of the sea and the wind wearing at the land. Think of the change in the continents and residents of countries through war and exodus. Continue to understand the changeable nature in the universe. See that the only stable law is that everything does change. Examine your disturbance. See the change in the disturbance.

Ask yourself, 'Is this disturbance caused by my inability to accept change?' Ask yourself, 'Do I cause this disturbance by not understanding that this subject is also subject to change?' The practitioner should continue with the contemplation until he is quite sure that he has learned to come to terms with the changing nature of the universe and that he is quite sure to the marrow that the subject of the disturbance is changing and temporary.

Contemplation on the Place of the Disturbance in the Scheme of Things

In this meditation, you wish to see the usefulness of this subject matter in the workings of existence. You want to see what useful function the disturbance fulfils in the grand scheme of things. This function, no matter how small and subtle, must be understood and accepted if the student is to achieve the object of this contemplation. The practitioner should imagine the whole of existence as a complex arrangement of moving parts, just like a set of cogs and wheel connecting.

The practitioner should understand that even the most detestable or useless part of existence serves a hidden purpose and needs to exist. For there to be light, there must be darkness. The practitioner must spend time looking at the subject matter that causes the disturbance. He must understand its place in existence. He must remain calm as with all other contemplation and understand both the place it has in the universe and the place it has in his life. He should see what he can learn from this disturbance. Or how it helps him to help others. The practitioner should spend time looking at the purpose of each small thing in the world from an ant to the gentle wind in spring until he is quite sure that everything, including his disturbance, has its place in the universe and should be accepted. The highly moral practitioner, of course, may find this hard and should always remember that acceptance is not condolence or recommendation.

Contemplation on the Empty Nature of Existence

This is the hardest of the contemplations. The practitioner should imagine that he is standing in the centre of existence. He should imagine all the planets and the stars in the whole of the universe. He should contemplate the space between the stars and planets. He should imagine the vast emptiness of existence. Imagine how the planets and stars are formed of the same energy. Imagine this mass of energy appearing in so many different forms. Imagine the earth and its inhabitants all formed from one great force. Imagine this force appearing in so many different ways, but its essence is a pure force without quality and colour. Imagine the whole of existence as an illusion. Think of your other meditations on time and change. The practitioner should continue this contemplation until he can see the ultimate emptiness and illusionary nature of his disturbance.

Control

Some aspects may be very deeply rooted or could be innately part of you. These disturbances may not respond to the methods above, though most do. If a disturbance will not respond to the above methods, it does not need to be resolved—it needs to be tamed! There are no underlying issues or unresolved conflicts. If there were, they might have disappeared, leaving the disturbance or incorrect thinking. The disturbance may even be a way of expressing to you that a new solution is needed. To control the disturbance, you need to take away the opportunity for its expression. If possible, remove yourself from the environments, the triggers and the routines that make this appear. Look at the outcome you have been seeking with your previous behaviour and find a way that brings around a superior result. Make sure that your new better expression has a reward and crowds out the previous way of doing things. Once you have this new routine in place hold firm and allow time to undertake its work.

BRINGING THE GOOD MIND INTO YOUR DAILY LIFE

CHAPTER 15

When you practice meditation, you create a template ideal consciousness, connecting with vibrations that will spread into your everyday awareness. This section contains methods of helping that blessing take route and how to use your daily life to align your consciousness with that ideal state.

The Rewards of Labour

Becoming more awake and more focused has its advantages but should be carefully managed. This section helps you deal with the new growth.

A Beautiful Garden

Imagine if you were left in charge of looking after a beautiful garden and was given sole responsibility for its cultivation and development. What would you do? Would you spend your time sitting in the garden as it became overgrown? Would you ignore the garden and leave it to its own devices? Would you abuse the land and use it for financial gain?

Most of us would answer that we would do our best to make that garden the most pleasant environment we could. We would utilise the natural surroundings, working with the tools and environment to make the garden as impressive and pleasant as possible. However, when it comes to the even more important responsibility of regulation and development of ourselves, a human rarely takes the same approach. In life, our situation is like the gardener—we are put in charge of ourselves.

This is a divine statement of responsibility. The very fact that we have been given by birth right responsibility for our mind, personality, and how we interact with the world is a strong statement regarding our duty in life. For most people, this is the only thing that Divine Providence says to us in our lifetime, 'You are in charge, do your best.'

Actions speak louder than words, and the message is quite clear. We are born with certain personal characteristics, but we should not accept our personality as it comes. Like the garden, we should view this as the raw material to work on and make it our life-long task to improve ourselves and overcome our faults.

The King and His Adviser

In the mystery schools of the past, the Initiate was taught the secrets of correct thinking. He was taught to be logical and distinguish truth from illusion. Even up to one hundred years ago, correct thinking and arts designed to produce mental balance were taught at universities. The Trivium (Grammar, Rhetoric, and Logic) and the Quadrivium (Geometry, Arithmetic, Music, and Astronomy) were taught, developing both sides of the human personality. Perhaps what we would call in modern terms the left and right brain. It will come as no surprise to the reader that mental health problems have risen so much in the last few decades since these arts have been forgotten. If people are not educated in correct thought, how can they be expected not to ever stray? Likewise, if people are encouraged to live their lives out of balance, dedicating so much attention to one area or another, then it is inevitable that the person's mind and personality will develop in a one-sided way. It is much like only exercising one side of the body.

Everything must be in balance in education and life. The two great pillars of King Solomon's Temple and the crook and flail of Osiris are clear statements that for humans, true balance is a harmony of opposites. This rule applies in all areas of human conduct. In our moral judgements, we must be as merciful as we are severe. Both principles are as important as each other. There must always be a carrot and a stick. In our personal development, we must look at our aims to motivate us and look at our past failures to prevent us from repeating mistakes. It is a great shame that it seems that humans, both as individuals and as a collective unit, cannot find such balance.

The student will notice a tendency in societies and individuals to forget the carrot or forget the stick. In our present world, we have gone full circle. First, we punished so terribly that we forgot to reward a change of character and give people a reason to be lawful. An eye for an eye was the cry, or as the Roman saying goes, 'Mentus improbs compescit, non clementia' (Fear, not kindness, restrains the wicked -Syrus Maxims). These sayings are very emotive but entirely incorrect from the Hermetic point of view. The truth is that both fear and kindness together in harmony are the only way to reform a man effectively. Nowadays, we are starting to forget that there must be a price to pay for immoral actions. There is again a Roman saying to illustrate this point: 'Dum vitant stulti vitia, in cintraria currunt' (When fools try to avoid a vice, they sometimes rush into its opposite—Horace, Satirae I,2,24). This is kind of like over-steering your car to compensate when you skid on ice. The student of Hermetics must take responsibility for his education in correct thought. He must keep his intellect and emotions in balance. He must also learn not to overcompensate when he sees a vice in himself or others. Whenever a human makes a decision, he bases it on two things: his reason and his emotions. It is the task of the student of Hermetics to make sure that he keeps these two forces in balance. The emotions and intellect (knowledge) should work in harmony. You should use your consciousness to keep the two in harmony.

Reason and emotions, however, are true opposites. Reason is naturally passive, and the emotions vie for attention and control. For true balance, the average human will have to develop his logical facilities and learn to understand and control his emotions. Likewise, all exercises in this volume should be practised in a balanced way. No area should surpass the other. True balance should be the aim of any serious practitioner. In this chapter, we are going to look at methods to adjust the mind and balance the temperament through adjustment in daily life. We will also discuss methods to retain this balance and prevent people and events from disturbing your equilibrium. Following this is an allegorical key to the exercises in this section. This analogy helps the student understand the correct relationship that the emotions, reason, and will should have.

The practitioner should read the following description several times if need be so that he or she is quite sure that it has become his mental property, as all the exercises that follow in this chapter rely on understanding this outlook.

In the human mind, there are two distinct thinking methods, or rather in the human psyche, we have two forms of mind. These are referred to as the conscious and unconscious mind in modern terms. In spiritual traditions throughout the world, these two minds have been likened to elements in nature. The Chinese call the conscious mind the Wisdom mind. This mind is the clear thinking, logical part of the human. It is also sometimes called the water mind because of its direct cool, rational, and tactical thinking. It always finds the easiest and most appropriate way of dealing with things.

In the Hermetic tradition, this mind is known as the King Mind or Ruling Mind. Like a king and wise ruler, it sits on the throne of judgement and makes decisions. Looking at the facts presented and using detached, logical thinking, King Solomon represents to the aspirant a high development of this mental ability.

Our other mind is the emotional mind or Fire mind. This is the unconscious mind of modern psychology. This mind is designed to warn us and advise us of how to react to given stimuli. The advice we are given comes from two sources. First, from our experiences of life and second from our instincts. Imagine that each of your emotions stands like advisers in the royal court. Our anger advises us on matters of war like an army general or military adviser. Our love pleads for us to help and care for others, like a social adviser. Our fear advises on areas to avoid and about possible dangers of any kind. Each emotion advises us on how to act. All our emotions are useful and worth listening to. Some spiritual paths preach the destruction of your emotions. These paths, in effect, are turning our troops on themselves.

Without advice from our emotions, life can be very hard. These people are throwing away thousands of years of human knowledge handed down by our ancestors and rejecting God-given reactions to danger. The point is to understand what our emotions are. They are advisers, and because of their limitations, they will offer advice in a limited way. Your anger will only ever suggest destruction. Your fear will suggest you run away. Your advisers learn by association and sometimes get things wrong! Likewise, sometimes we are born with or develop an adviser that always wants to be heard. The angry man has a military adviser who sees war as the answer to all problems. The trick is to know your advisers and to deal with them as a king would. Learn to listen to them but never be controlled by them! Another set of advisers to be discussed are our instincts.

Advice from our animal instincts can often cause problems in day to day life. Our mind draws on thousands of years of evolution to be able to advise us in this manner. These advisers stand like old sages in the courtroom of our minds. Their advice is based on the most critical elects of survival and living and usually is very useful. However, their advice is often outdated and can cause problems in the modern world. The same stress response that was very useful for our ancestors to get away from their enemy is not a helpful response to a hefty bill or parking ticket. Mental illnesses in humans are frequently caused by these two minds coming into conflict and far more rarely by organic disorders of the physical brain.

REGULATING AND BALANCING THE MIND

CHAPTER 16

To keep a healthy and balanced mind, as you go about your daily business, you will notice the two minds in you, or rather you will notice when you change your method of thinking. Three principles should always be borne in mind. All three principles are interconnected and interrelated, as the reader will note.

1. You are the Lord of Your Mind and Actions

For you to make any progress in mental control, you must have a firm conviction in your mental prowess. You must have total belief in your ability to rule your mind. Any other thinking method or point of view is merely giving away control of your mind. The simplest way of becoming the master of your mind is to know yourself to be so. It is a well-known that a belief in one's abilities is needed to master almost any skill. If you doubt yourself, your mind will not be entirely focused on the job at hand. Your doubt will hinder you. As your doubts come from the emotional mind, you have given up your throne to what should have been your adviser—i.e., your emotions. Remember, as the lord of your mind, you must never give up your throne to your advisers. You must always be in control if you wish to retain your kingdom!

Anyone who has ever suffered from a panic attack will understand this mechanism. As soon as you realise that this feeling of panic can happen, or should I say as soon as someone believes that this feeling of panic can arise, at any moment, a horrific cycle is created. Panic attacks usually are triggered initially by some disturbing thought or event. Still, after the initial terrible experience has passed, the sufferer believes that they are no longer in control of themselves. They worry that they will panic in a public place or in front of other people. They believe that this process is beyond their control and are so scared by this that they reproduce the panic through worry simply because they believe they have lost control of themselves.

Always remember that you are the master of your mind and your thoughts. You are the king or queen of your mind. God has granted you the power of free will. Let nothing take that from you. Everything that you do is under your control. You can stand strong against anything that life throws at you and retain control. It is your divine right to do so.

2. Your 'Advising' Mind is Always Trying to Help You

No matter what situation you experience in life, your emotions are trying to give you the best advice they can. In every habit, in every mental illness, there is a gain. Your mind usually is scared and trying to protect you from something. The urge to drink alcohol comes from the emotional mind of an individual trying to protect themselves from life or his emotions. A nervous stammer could possibly protect us from saying something. Behind every emotional thought, there is an aim. Your royal court advisers have given you a suggestion. Sometimes it can come from a single adviser, such as a single emotion.

For example, when you are trying to find a parking space to park your car and you start to get angry, your anger is telling you that it thinks that aggression is the way out of this situation. You, however, know that this is not good advice. A more drastic example is that of persistent urges to do something or worry about something.

In this case, often the whole board of advisers has decided on the course of action that they think is best. However, the power to overcome these problems lies in the knowledge that it is nothing more than a suggestion. There is no reason why you should act on this advice if you know it to be incorrect. So, from now on in day to day life, if you have thoughts that worry or upset you, relax—don't let the thoughts disturb or control you.

Think of yourself as the king or queen on your throne, listening to your adviser. Try to look at the thought or emotion and see what the advice is about. If this emotional thought is misplaced, produce a rational alternative to this thought – one that you know will serve the purpose better. When you have decided on your solution, stick to it. If the emotional thoughts persist, again take the attitude of a king to his adviser and stick with your solution. You will not be badgered into anything.

Remember – YOU are the master of your mind.

Keep correcting your mind every time the thought reappears. It matters not if you need to correct your mind one time or one hundred times over this matter. The important thing is that you keep control and replace the suggestion with a better alternative.

CHAPTER 16: REGULATING AND BALANCING MIND

3. You Must Never Let Yourself be Overwhelmed by Your Emotions

This is a very important point.

A practitioner once said to me, 'Make it a secret principle never to let your mind be detained by any of the 10,000 things you perceive with your five senses!' The modern world is full of highly emotive things designed to get our attention. Billboards with sexual images are used for advertising, and soap operas have violent and nasty storylines. Never before have humans been exposed to such a high level of information.

When your emotions are captivated, you are being controlled. Your advisers are being influenced. Learn to detach and cut down the emotional white noise in your life. Save your energy for more enjoyable things. Remember how much time your ancestors were forced to rest before the invention of the electrical light, and compare how much time you rest now. You must remain calm and unmoved by your emotions and by emotional things. You must stand firm like a tree. For if your emotions control you, you will be scared of what you might say or do. The man who lives in fear of himself never gets a chance to rest. This is not to say that you cannot experience your emotions. You should never repress or cut out any emotion. You should allow yourself to experience the emotion but use your ruling mind to decide if and how you react to it. This is the correct way for humans to live and think. This way you can experience the fullness of life but also protect yourself from the events and evil in the world.

Never let yourself be overwhelmed by your emotions. If you do, you are letting one of your court advisers take your throne. The practitioner will now understand the true punishment that immoral people receive. The more someone lives by their selfish impulses, the weaker they become at resisting them. Soon the advisers have held a coup, and the person's mind is no longer his own. His internal devils sit on the throne controlling his destiny. He is now their servant. As the Egyptian saying goes,

> *Yield not to emotion, for there are discarnate forces around us who desire emotional existence. In the heat of passion, one surrenders to the influence of these. Ill health and unwise living are the result. Through firm instruction, one can master ones' emotions and these forces. In this make them serve one; thus the slave becomes the master.*

ADJUSTMENT OF THE MIND THROUGH ADJUSTMENT OF ONE'S SPEECH

CHAPTER 17

In the modern world, we live in a throwaway society. Everything is disposable. Products are now made to be disposable even when long-lasting designs have been proven to work in the past. This way, people keep having to buy and the economy benefits. The same is true of speech. Speech has become disposable and short term. Never before in the history of man has there been such a level of pointless, meaningless speech.

People have learned to talk for the sake of talking. Speech, like a currency, has been devalued. The value of taciturnity has become forgotten. Our speech is not merely background noise or monkey chatter. It is an expression of our will of sentiments. It is a powerful force that shapes both our mind and the mind of others. In this chapter, we will focus on the former.

The Power of Silence

Don't give too much of your force away. The power of silence has been known throughout the ages. All traditions allude to the hidden power of silence. When we talk, we let our emotions flow out of us. When humans have a passion or emotion, they are compelled to release it by action or word. When the emotion is expressed the emotion dissipates. The tentative reader will realise how this mechanism is used to relieve suffering. For example, when one talks of negative emotions, we feel temporarily relieved, as in therapeutic counselling.

Herein lies the weakness of free and easy talk. If one expresses one's passions through profuse and zealous speech, we temporarily release our need for expression or action. Or as the great Jewish wise man Shammai stated, 'Say little and do much! The righteous say little and do much, but the wicked say much and do little.'

The point made here is clear. For humans, there are two main methods of self-expression words or actions. You must choose your ratio wisely. In silence lies strength. The expression of the strong, silent type is no mistake. A calm, silent person has a far better ability to carry a high workload because he has greater emotional reserves to express himself in this manner.

Don't give too much of yourself away. If you talk excitedly about your hobbies and interests, you will find that when it comes time to do the activity, you have used up your enthusiasm for the subject. Many people take advantage of this on both the emotional and spiritual level. People leech off the force of others' excitement while never giving anything away from themselves.

Don't Devalue the Currency

For a healthy and happy life, you need to be able to communicate well with others. When you talk too much, you devalue what you say. People stop listening to you and taking what you say seriously.

As the ancient Egyptian saying states:

Speak not too much for men are deaf to the man of many words, be silent rather, then shalt you please, therefore speak not, before all thing guard they speech, for a man's' ruin lie in his tongue. The human is a storehouse full of all manner of answers. Choose therefore the right one and let the rest remain imprisoned in the body. When you talk too much, you devalue what you say, and in extreme cases, you may as well be mute for all the attention people pay to your advice.

Or, as the Biblical saying goes,

The mouth of the just bringeth forth wisdom, but the forward tongue will be cut off.

If you are taciturn and you choose your words carefully, people will unconsciously understand that your words stand for something. People will listen to what you say. Your emotions will remain calm and pure. Careless talk is the most common cause of social strife. The practitioner understanding these things can imbalance the mind and will do his best to avoid such torments.

The ancient Egyptians advise us to, 'Put a bridle on the tongue, set a guard before thy lips, lest the word of thine own mouth destroy thy peace. On much speaking cometh repentance, but in silence is safety', and 'If you meet a disputant who is your equal, you

CHAPTER 17: ADJUSTMENT OF THE MIND THROUGH ADJUSTMENT OF ONE'S SPEECH

will overcome them with silence while they speak evilly. Those who witness the encounter will remark on this and your name will be held in high esteem among the great.'

Keep Silent About Holy Things

Never permit anyone to look into your sanctuary. Keep divine matters hermetically sealed in your breast. When you talk about sacred things, you debase them. You transform them into something mundane. This transformation takes place on three levels. First of all, in the minds and spirits of those listening to you. You give them the message that these things are not to be treated with respect. This is the hidden message in the Biblical quote, 'The fear of God is the root of wisdom.' You also risk the disapproval and disbelief of others if you talk to them about spiritual matters. In a society that has little or no faith in such things, your mind may become influenced by the words of others. The disbelief also influences you on a spiritual level, especially if the person is very emotive on the subject. No practitioner wants the disbelief of others to affect him in such an adverse way. Remember, once someone knows something, it may often be in their mind, so it is an ongoing problem. If you can't control your tongue, how can you expect the person that you are telling to do so! This is how the problem spreads.

As the great adept Jesus said,

Cast not your pearls before swine lest they trample them underfoot.

Secondly, the talk also affects your mind. Your higher aspirations and will become dissipated and de sanctified by everyday speech. Your deeper mind will lose its reverence for such matters. This may cause you to relax your discipline or not put the required effort into your Hermetic exercises. The ancient Egyptians advise us,

The abomination of the sanctuary of God is too much talking. Pray you with a loving heart the petitions of which are all secret, God will do thy business, hear that which you say and will accept thine offering.

Worse is for social reasons if you have to talk against your beliefs, as this will cause doubts to arise in your mind.

Thirdly and perhaps the most important matter is that of the interaction between you and Divine Providence. The divine way opens most to those who are silent. By remaining silent on all spiritual matters, you avoid the deception pride can cause. Too often, people use their spiritual path to encase their sense of self. Under these conditions, what can result but a strong need to achieve for the sake of the show. Slowly the practitioner will become more and more comfortable with boasting of their achievements and pretending to gain results. Before long, they may not even know what is true and what is not. Any true practitioner will understand how imagination is such a part of the magical process that no other motives must become involved. In addition to the above, you will shatter your divine links if you ground yourself by realising the force through speech. As the ancient Egyptian saying goes,

> *Be still and solemn silence keep, then shall god open the way for salvation. Withdraw into thyself and father-mother god will come. Throw away the work of the body's sensations thy divinity will come to birth, purge from thyself the animal torments, concerns with things of matter.*

The divine forces only open to those of a trustworthy nature. As the Biblical saying goes,

> *A talebearer revealeth secrets but he that is of a faithful spirit concealeth the matter. You must prove you are worthy of the holy mysteries of nature and divinity by retaining your silence on these matters.*

You Scatter Thoughts with Uncontrolled Words

Careless and uncontrolled talk scatters your thoughts and alters the programs in your mind. We all know that if we hear something said a large number of times, we start to believe the statement. Modern science has proven the effectiveness of both autosuggestion and subliminal suggestion. Subliminal suggestions are so effective that use for advertising has been banned in England. In Hermetic wisdom, we know of two circuits of thought in the mind each with power to program thought. The first circuit is simply thought known as the lesser circuit. Whenever we think something, the thought starts from an intent in the person.

The intent is like the fuse on a firework that once lit, the thought is due to come. Then the thought runs through the various mental processes, moving in a complete circuit back to the point of intent. Each time this happens, the intention becomes stronger, and the particular line of thought becomes easier to repeat. When the line of thinking has become so strong that it almost happens without any effort (i.e., the intent and its release have become so strong that they dominate), we call this a habit. This principle can be used to great advantage. As the saying goes, 'Practice makes perfect.' We all instinctively know that the more we do something, the easier it becomes. The same is true of thought. The more we think a certain way, the easier it is to think that way. Here lies the root of the problems of obsession. This also lies in the effectiveness of visualisation and mental rehearsal and, for the most part, hypnotherapy.

However, the second and more powerful circuit is that of speech. When you speak, first you have your intent, then think of what to say. Then you coordinate your mouth and vocal cords to speak. While you talk, you hear the noises that you make, and your mind interprets them as words and understands the meaning. Two circuits work at the same time. You trigger the thought circuit (the lesser circuit) and a circuit of reinforcement caused by the effort speech and the reception and understanding of speech.

CHAPTER 17: ADJUSTMENT OF THE MIND THROUGH ADJUSTMENT OF ONE'S SPEECH

Most important of all, you hear yourself saying what you say. The more important the person's opinion is, the more effective their words tend to have on you, so what you hear yourself saying is very important.

Here lies the truth in the Chinese saying,

He who knows does not speak.
He who speaks does not know.
One must close one's mouth
And shut one's gate,
Blunt one's sharp wit,
Dissolve ones confused thoughts
Moderate one's light,
Make one's earthiness common.[4]

When you talk, you program your mind so what you say will become real opinions of yourself if you keep repeating them. Your emotions will also become raised, and you may find that they take you over in heated discussion. Be careful to talk in a well thought out, calm manner. Communication is important and enjoyable. Just avoid saying things you don't believe and remember the Egyptian saying,

It is better to either be silent, or to say things of more value than silence, sooner throw a pearl at a hazard than an idle or useless word and do not say little with many words, but a great deal with few.

Baby Tigers

One of the most important skills on the path to self-mastery is learning to stop things when they are small and weak. For example, if your habit is to lust after other women or watch pornographic films. You may think that this habit in itself will not cause problems, especially if your wife has no objections. But as a natural tendency, it will grow. The more you give into unfaithful thoughts, imaginings, and indulgences, the more you will want. Your urge to be unfaithful will not be realised by these actions but will instead grow. Remember, you always get more of what you focus on. On a smaller level, it is like buying a baby tiger or crocodile. It looks really cute and like a wonderful idea, but it will grow up in time. Some readers may find this idea amusing, but many people in London have indeed bought such animals and been surprised when the animal gets so large that it tries to eat them. The sewers of London are said to be full of crocodiles that are dumped as a result of this kind of stupidity. We all laugh at such folly, but the truth is as clear as can be seen. We all often make this kind of silly mistake with our own lives and habits.

---

[4]Tao Te Ching #56

We can all see the kind of habits that lead to worse and larger sins. The most important point to remember is if you partly fulfil a deep urge or desire with a seemingly harmless habit, be careful you are very sure this is not a baby tiger that is going to grow up and eat you.

Correct your mind as you would your posture.

HOW TO TURN PROCRASTINATION AND INNER CONFLICT TO YOUR ADVANTAGE

CHAPTER 18

It is early morning and the alarm sounds, reminding you it is time to get up to do your practice—be it yoga, meditation, or to go for a run. This is a goal you have thought about and have decided that you want to do. When you went to bed, you were determined you would get up and spring into action, yet the warmth of the bed calls, and you find it difficult to motivate yourself to get up. You may find all manner of inner objections rise to try and prevent you from fulfilling your chosen goal. Perhaps a more agreeable and easier suggestion will come to mind as a way to put off the goal until later. It is that moment of inner conflict that I call the sticking point.

It is this aspect we will be looking at and how we can turn internal objections, or sticking points, around to be used for our empowerment. That moment, instead of being a roadblock in your attempt to fulfil your goal, it can be flipped and become a moment you can push off from, using the energy to create momentum to achieve your goal. These techniques can be used for any form of discipline. Not only can they be used with an ongoing activity such as meditation practice, exercise, or study, but this approach can also be used for mundane or tedious tasks such as accounts.

Let us imagine that you decide to tackle an activity on Sunday afternoon. However, when Sunday afternoon arrives suddenly you find that there are all sorts of reasons why you should put it off until later or even next week. You are reminded that you have friends that want to see you, or perhaps you have something far more compelling that draws you away from your intended activity. Soon you find yourself being pulled away from the task, so what can you do to stay on target?

The first stage in overcoming the objections that prevent you from carrying out your will is to identify each one and which ones tend to win. Then you can tackle the objection using the method best suited. You will find that they come in three broad categories.

1. A Confused Approximation of the Goal

This is where an alternative is offered to the original goal with the suggestion that it is not really an alternative, but that it does fulfil the original aim. An example of this could be a person deciding to do their morning meditation routine lying down rather than sitting up as they usually would. There could be all sorts of justifications, but the truth is this person is looking to avoid getting out of bed.

If this happens to you, next time pay careful attention and you will find there is a small moment of rational thought that informs you of the true intention. In the above example, there is likely to be a flash of insight that by taking that course of action, the person will most likely fall asleep, not meditate. But then the inner conflict comes up with a rational argument as to why this would be acceptable approach and proceeds to convince the mind that meditating in bed is a good idea. For someone wanting to exercise each morning, they may find themselves reasoning, 'Well, I walked around town all day yesterday so, I do not feel it is necessary to go for a run this morning because I already exercised. I will sleep in.'

This kind of reasoning is a confused approximation since the mind tries to convince us that the replacement activity is equivalent to the original. This works exceptionally well when we have mixed intentions about the initial goal. From outside, it is plain to see that these suggestions are irrational and seem somewhat ridiculous to us; however, the mind can be extremely creative when it comes to procrastination.

Overcoming this barrier has a lot to do with not giving it time to get a hold. But first, identify whether there is a genuine reason. If, for example, you are finding it difficult to do your morning routine because you always find yourself tired in the morning, consider whether you should be going to bed earlier. Next, make sure the goal is very clearly defined in your mind and what would constitute success. Be cautious to ensure it is achievable. Once you have done this, you will find it easier to move your focus back on track. You can use the approximation as a reminder to focus on the purpose and value in your goal, and in this way, you will find it aids your motivation.

2. Negative Self-Speak

This one is self-explanatory. Rather than encouraging yourself, your self-speak, it will demotivate and belittle you and your efforts.

Here is a list of some examples:

- I can't do this
- It won't make any difference, so why am I bothering?
- I will only fail

CHAPTER 18: HOW TO TURN YOUR PROCRASTINATION AND INNER CONFLICT TO YOUR ADVANTAGE

- I am stupid for even thinking this was a good idea in the first place
- I was never the clever one at school, so I won't pass the exam
- I will only make myself look like a fool

You know you are in this category when the main reason for not attempting to go through with the activity is an overwhelmingly negative feeling and, in extreme cases, self-loathing. This isn't just shown just in the words said, but also in the tone used and images that may manifest.

One way to test this is to imagine if you would use the same phrasing and tone to someone else in a similar circumstance. If this was your best friend attempting to improve their life, then would you say the same things? This exercise sometimes exposes just how tough we are on ourselves.

The best way to tackle negative self-speak is first to change the tone used. This can be done in two ways. Sometimes simply changing the tone will make the statement supportive. 'Come on,' for example, can be said disparagingly and sarcastically to discourage you from the action. Yet by changing the tone, it becomes encouraging and supportive. However, if the wording itself cannot be altered, then adjust the tone to take power away from the voice. Mickey Mouse is a particularly good choice for this since it is hard to take anything he may say particularly seriously! Use this as a way to practice self-speak and correct your inner voice to the ideal tone. In this way, you will gain an inner supporter and ally.

3. Dismissal of the Goal

The rationalisation by the mind of why a particular goal should not be completed can be quite creative, and sometimes it can take some careful analysing and unravelling to see the truth. Below are some excuses you may have encountered. We will look at each one to determine what the reality of the situation is and how to bring yourself back on target.

One common excuse is finding a reason for why today an exception and the goal is in some way harmful or counterproductive. For example, 'I was ill last night, so I won't run today. Better to rest when you are ill, so I recover quickly and then can run once I'm better.' In this case, the reason given is that by running the person will make themselves feel worse, and the implication is that by not running today, they will be able to run sooner. However, often the reality is that our inner conflict colours our assessment of the situation. In the warm bed, we decide we are too ill to get up and go outside where it is cold, choosing instead to stay tucked in. If we got up and ready to go, then we would be in a better position to decide whether the concern is legitimate.

Rather than using the objection as a reason to stop training, it can be used to enhance our discipline. Training is most valuable under adversity since life rarely stops, and when we train, we are practising for real life. So, if you are ill and concerned that a run would be too tough, then go for a therapeutic walk. If you feel tired and are concerned you will not be able to meditate, then use that tiredness as your training. Learning to focus through fatigue is a vital skill practised in different spiritual traditions throughout the world.

One reason students often give for avoiding a particular exercise is that they have in some way already completed it; they are now on to higher and more complicated things. Counter-intuitively, you will find the more challenging the undertaking, the more likely some people will decide that it is too easy as a means not to do it. By determining, 'I have already learned this, it is beneath me,' they are avoiding the risk of failure without admitting weakness. The easiest way to counter this is to turn the argument on its head, to say, 'If this is so easy, then it will be no bother for me to do it.' If you find yourself still resistant, then you may have found the area you need to work on the hardest.

To Review

1. Are you coming up with some plan that involves a change to what you said you were going to do?
2. Are you talking to yourself negatively?
3. Are you coming up with rationalisations for not doing it at all?

Once these patterns of behaviour have been identified, it becomes easier to know which areas need a degree of focus. This becomes a wonderful form of training whereby you use these very objections as your motivation. Think of a martial artist who uses the strength of an opponent to twist around and throw him. As you practice, you will find the negative-speak, approximation, or the rationalisation of dismissal starts lessening. If you find yourself procrastinating about achieving that goal and putting it off till tomorrow, then the time to act is NOW. Say to yourself, I am going to do this NOW.'

When faced with a creative solution, be sure to turn the logic around on itself. If you decide, 'I am going to do my meditation in bed because it's harder,' instead question the logic. It's not harder. Otherwise, you would up already and practising. If it feels harder to get up, then use the primary reason for staying in bed to motivate you to get up. Let us challenge ourselves then and do what is more difficult.

Or, if the task seems too easy, then perhaps think to yourself, 'If I am a great master, then this should be a triviality. Let's just do it.' The key is to make the objection part of the solution. With practice, you will find your way of converting whatever your negative or internal objections are into positive outcomes. This allows us to override our negative programming.

Awareness of Consequences

Another powerful method that can be employed is to associate the negativity with the consequences of failing to do the action. However, it is important to keep this as a healthy motivator to ensure the goal is achieved, as it can easily move into harmful areas.

In an ideal world, we would only ever use positive motivators. If we were trying to eat more healthily, then we may remind ourselves that healthy eating means that we have

CHAPTER 18: HOW TO TURN YOUR PROCRASTINATION AND INNER CONFLICT TO YOUR ADVANTAGE

more energy to do the things we love. However, the mind often leans towards more of a negative focus. If this is carefully controlled, then it can be used to your benefit. For example, if we are trying to eat more healthily because the doctor has warned us that we are at risk of a heart attack, then we use that as a reminder when we are thinking of deviating from the goal.

But, as I said before, it is important to be careful with this approach. For some people, this can very easily become negative self-speak. This is especially true for those who already have tendencies towards negative self-speak and shouldn't be used by them. An example where this has gone wrong would be if we started to attack our image or personality, trying to shame ourselves into eating healthier. This can be successful in the short term, but over time becomes a very unproductive approach. If you find yourself doing this, then I recommend you avoid this course of action altogether. It is not a good long-term method, because you are programming the negative self-speak into your consciousness. Remember, always associate the negative outcome to the negativity that is getting in the way. This is a very important principle to note because then the association remains correct, and your positive action is clear and free from negative emotional attachment.

INNER ALCHEMY

CHAPTER 19

As your daily meditation deepens, you will find yourself naturally finding ways to turn all hardships and limitations to blessings and opportunities. In this chapter, I will give some examples of the kind of transformations and evolutions that are possible as you turn base metals into gold within your consciousness.

Making Friends with Negative Emotions

Our emotions are important signals never to be ignored. As previously mentioned, we can imagine them like advisers in a royal court. If you imagine yourself as the king or queen in your castle and each one of your emotions has a different advisory role within the court.

Anger

Could be likened to a war minister who advises on what threats we must eliminate, defend against, or deal with.

Sadness

Could be in charge of memorials and of things we need to pay our respects to. It could also help us to be aware of the aspects of our lives that are important to us, and we would miss if they were to go too.

Fear

Could be the minister of protection, informing us of danger and risks to our health and those around us—a kind of health and safety report on life.

Jealousy

Could be the minister of equality, helping to ensure that we are treated fairly in relation to others. Jealousy also reminds us of what we find important and how to spend our resources.

As you can see, our emotions are important, and we need to learn to listen to them. However, they should have the same position in our minds as I have just described in the royal court. Each emotion is there to offer advice and advice only. It should never take the throne. Therefore no one emotion should ever be in control, but each one should always be listened to.

Likewise, it is essential to learn to understand your own emotions. Only when you take the time to listen and understand your emotions will you know which ones are to be trusted and which emotions are often incorrect or overreact. That way, it is possible to learn to interact with them in a very healthy way.

If you have a persistent emotion that will not fade or disappear, often this is because we have yet to solve the problem it is warning us about. The result of this is usually that the emotion, in an attempt to be heard, starts to shout louder, maybe even seizing the throne if these emotions are not appropriately addressed. Rather than deal with them, often we employ all sorts of strange methods to get rid of them. People may resort to taking pills as a way of suppressing emotions. Another tactic is to push unwanted emotions to one-side and use distraction to ignore them, rather than listen and find out the cause of the disturbance. When we are feeling stressed or upset, we may turn on the TV to take our mind off it or go for a drink with friends. All of these methods of avoidance are employed as a way of crowding out the emotions. It is like having a warning light come on in your car, and, instead of dealing with the problem, a piece of tape is placed over it.

In truth, we don't want our emotions to stop giving us feedback. Instead, we want them to inform us of relevant information since they are our warning lights. But we do need to be able to view the advice clearly and act appropriately. The function of the emotions is to aid and inform us when something is needing our attention. As we learn to listen to them, we begin to find out the true reasons behind their expression. We then gain the ability to understand them more and allow them to be expressed in an integrated and harmonious way.

Letting Go of Status, Pride and Selfish Ambition

Much importance is placed on status and vying for position and success in society. I believe these things are mental hindrances. Perhaps if we were to reject all titles, qualifications, and physical symbols of rank, class, and wealth to focus on the things we genuinely want to do with our lives, then we would have a refreshing sense of freedom.

The longer I spend contemplating society, the more I am convinced that most of us spend our entire lives in struggle. We desperately try to build a sense of self without realising that it is all temporary, that what we are putting our time and effort into will only disappear. It is far more important to let go of this futile task, this building up of something that can't be maintained, and to instead focus on the more essential aspects of life. You cannot make yourself so important, so special, that you don't die. All that will remain is your effect on the world—the fruits of your labours.

Train Your Mind as You Would Your Body

Wouldn't it be wonderful if we trained our minds like we train our bodies? If you visit the gym, you will see a vast array of different types of training equipment. Treadmills, cardiovascular machines, and cycles for training your heart and lungs. Weights to lift and train your supporting muscles. There are machines where you can focus on pure strength. Nowadays, gyms tend to have lots of innovative functional apparatus that allow you to train your body to be able to apply the training to real life. If you look at us as a race, you can see that we all instinctively know that physical exercise can heal us. If we injure a part of our body, the very first thing we do is start to move it, to check out where the injury is, and to establish the problem area. We then begin to look for ways to fix it and we are happy to share such knowledge. So, if we have bad posture or a sore back, we recommend to each other particular exercises which will help correct the injury or one which repeats the correct type of movement. We are happy to adjust our posture in daily life and change the way we move.

If we would do the same with our minds, I think the world would be a very different place. Imagine a world where it was normal to practice changing your state of mind, to train it to work better in your daily life. For example, you could practice dealing with depression by setting a timer and seeing how long you can feel happy about something and keep practising improving your skill, working up second by second. Imagine a circumstance where we change our attitude just like we change our posture, where we train our mental strength, flexibility, and coordination just the same as we train our physical bodies.

In society, there is a bit of a taboo about mental illness, so we are less likely to talk to people about our emotional problems than if we had a sore knee. But what if we approach these two problems in the same way? Perhaps there is an emotion that you feel very uncomfortable with or find very hard to experience. To strengthen the emotion, you would need to practice experiencing it to help bring it into balance. For example, if you found it hard to cry, you could watch sad films or read old Greek tragedies. In this way, you would be able to heal it or become proficient in expressing that emotion. I think this would bring balance to ourselves and thus to our society.

Contemplate this suggestion and look at any areas in your mental functioning that you believe could be improved. Think about how you train them and how you can improve them the same way you would train something to do with the body. This approach, I believe, can lead to a greater balance that will spread out from ourselves to the rest of the world.

The Seed of Something Beautiful

I have come to believe some of our worst qualities and greatest vices are the seeds of our most important virtues, our highest potential, and all we need to do is to learn how to cultivate those seeds and help them mature into what they are meant to be.

If you ask someone to do something difficult for them, or very new, they will often find an approximation of their intended goal. This may occur with someone who starts to learn yoga but is new to exercise and therefore lacking in flexibility. If they attempt to perform a posture which requires them to put their arms over their head, they may find that they do not have the range of movement to comfortably bring their arms straight above their head and so the hands will be out of alignment. To compensate, they may well angle the hands up and will be convinced that they are performing the correct posture. Often, they are not aware of this and feel the goal has been achieved. They may inadvertently hurt themselves while thinking they are improving their health. It would be wrong to stop them from practising because of this. Instead, it would be better to encourage them to continue developing their practice until it becomes what they were aiming for all along.

This is also evident in life. We tend to work according to our nature, and we often choose careers that reflect that. However, if we are given a task that is outside our remit of experience, we often use our previous experience and a way we already know works. So, to use a method that we know works for us to achieve the intended goal, we change it to suit our nature. For example, if we are asked to do a job that involves a lot of stamina and meticulous attention, but our natural strengths are of a more energetic and strong nature, we may perform the task with haste. Although we complete it, we are likely to miss the important details required for the completion of the task to the same standard that a slower and more detailed person would reach.

Often our negative expressions are due to the fact we have yet to develop the required skills in that area. To compensate, we apply the same old strategies for dealing with new situations but find that they do not work, and this may produce an adverse reaction or feeling.

As we grow and develop, we realise that certain situations require certain responses that are appropriate for that moment. To illustrate, being assertive in a business environment is necessary to achieve results, but not helpful when dealing with a mourning relative, which requires a degree of tact and gentleness. If we have not developed the ability to adapt to different environments, we may find it challenging to switch between different modes of behaviour. This lack of flexibility can often be perceived as a negative quality, but in truth, the individual has yet to learn the necessary skill. Perhaps in this situation, they have not yet realised that assertiveness is not always the best way to bring someone's focus away from a negative emotion outside of the working environment, and the importance of being gentle and kind.

Inflammation in the body is analogous to this. The body experiences inflammation when it perceives a foreign entity, or when the body becomes injured, it acts as a way to protect itself from further harm. However, if this intention becomes misplaced, an autoimmune response will activate whereby the body starts to attack itself, thinking its cells are the foreign entity. So the body is doing its best to protect itself, but it has made an error. The personality operates similarly. It may act in a way that it thinks is beneficial, but in fact, works more of a hindrance to the outcome it is trying to create.

An example of this would be someone who genuinely wants people to respect them. They want to set an example and to be of benefit to the world, to be the person others see doing the right thing. This expression may manifest in the desire to become famous at all costs. In another circumstance, maybe someone wishes to create a beautiful environment for people and wants to make the world a better place. They also wish to protect the people they love around them. This desire for beauty may direct them onto a path focused on obtaining wealth to fulfil their goal. However, they have forgotten that happiness is the true desire behind their original intention, but become focused on creating a grandiose environment. We all know examples of business people who have made vast amounts of money, yet if you ask why they are still chasing bigger profits and bonuses, they say it is for the home and family. In reality, the family has been taken care of, but what is lacking is love, time, and presence.

Sometimes, what is a normal positive emotion can turn into a perceived negative one due to an inner confusion. Perhaps the desire to avoid an expression of emotion is a way of dealing with an aspect of life that they find difficult. This is often due to a past negative experience that has imprinted itself onto the mind, and now any experience related to that emotion becomes blanketed with the same negativity. An example of this may be someone who has a perceived negative view of having sexual relations with another person and chooses to renounce this aspect of their life. They decide to be celibate rather than engaging in healthy relationships, maybe to avoid the emotional pain or discomfort that they feel surrounding that area in their life.

In some cases, a person may have been hurt emotionally by others in the past saying negative things. A decision is made to join a silent monastic order to avoid dealing with negative interactions. In this case, that person should learn how to deal with the negativity from others to conquer these aspects of their personality. The lesson is about empowerment and developing new skills in dealing with life. The personality will often try to find an easy option, an approximation of the goal because it is a challenge and requires effort to transcend that undeveloped aspect of the personality.

In conclusion, it is understood that the goal is to master these aspects of our personality. To find the genuine cause that lies behind our expression. It is that seed, or beautiful spark, which is our true intention. So often our experiences and emotions colour, misdirect or confuse the manifestation of this intention, but hidden is a seed of our true potential. By finding the true purpose of our actions, we skilfully learn to understand our emotions and learn how to give them the highest expression they deserve.

Remember, all emotions have a purpose and find ways to express themselves because they are trying to communicate something significant to us about the situation we are in. This is true even of emotions we tend to label as negative. Just like the warning light in a car, we do not want to hide the warning but solve the problem. So, it is with an emotion—we need to listen to that signal and address it so that it can be expressed correctly. Often this means pausing rather than following your first instinct, which may be inappropriate and lead away from a good outcome.

In this way, we look at what the real purpose behind the emotion is and to utilise that. With this approach, we gain the most significant benefit, and this may be the only approach that leads to complete integration in the end.

Being Open to the Changes You Are Trying to Make

When we work consciously to evolve our lives or selves, we need to be open to change. This is true whether we are looking to build success, healing, inner tranquillity, or contentment. It is important to remember, if you have chosen this as your goal and it is something that is generally lacking in your life, then your habits, views of the world, and internal mechanisms will not be setup to achieve it. These need to change.

Think of these new habits as forming the vessel that can hold the new way and maintain it. Without these changes, the support is not in place, so we do not realise this transformation, or it slips through our fingers almost as soon as we grasp it. There are various reasons for this. It is not rare for someone who is creating success through energy work and visualisation to continually turn down paid work or business opportunities, which will lead to great wealth for minimal effort, as they are looking for their 'magical' solution. People who are working on calmness will sometimes find themselves rejecting situations that will lead to inner tranquillity as, without the internal change, they cannot recognise the solution or find it too uncomfortable. It is said that to those who are ill, medicine often looks like poison at first appearances. In some cases, a person who is ill may reject the medicine offered three or four times before accepting it.

Let us imagine that someone who has terrible arthritic problems is offered a place on a course of hydrotherapy. Due to the nature of the illness, it is quite hard for them to be motivated. In this situation, to get out of bed, to catch the bus, and to journey to the swimming pool requires great effort. They might even find themselves fearful of going through the pain that is involved in rehabilitation.

To grasp these opportunities, we first need to accept there is a need for change, a change of internal habits and lifestyle. Often, we find the most unexpected changes lead to the solution. Sometimes it's in the small changes to our attitude or perception that offers us the most significant benefits, not in the big ones. Often these opportunities are a chance to alter our perception. If you are doing everything to create that change, be ready to grasp it when it comes along in real life.

CHAPTER 19: INNER ALCHEMY

How to Enjoy More in Life

No matter who you are, the circumstances of your life, or where you are in the world, there are certain tasks that you have to do every day. Of course, some of these tasks are more enjoyable than others. But what if it is possible to find joy in every thought, word, and action?

The important key to obtaining this state is to understand that much of our enjoyment is circumstantial. It is more dependent on how we interpret the situation around us than we may at first realise. For instance, someone somewhere is in a classroom sitting in detention and having to write lines of sentences as a form of punishment. They hate every moment of it. After they have completed the page, they take it to the teacher, who looks at the lines before declaring they are not neat enough and sends them back to their desk to do it again. They feel very hurt and do not enjoy having to repeat this action. Yet, somewhere else, another person is paying for a calligraphy class, whereby they are beautifully creating letters. They, on the other hand, are enjoying every moment of that class. As they form each letter, they love the adjustments and improvements suggested to them. Like before, they take the completed sheet to their teacher, who, upon seeing the work, instructs them to repeat it. And they do so, loving the meditative nature of this continual improvement.

You may be able to see this interesting phenomenon in your own life as well. If you know someone who is really into physical fitness, maybe they do CrossFit or go to the gym regularly. You will most likely see a difference in attitude towards physical exertion dependent on the context. If you phone them to suggest meeting up and doing some great functional training together, they will most likely eagerly accept. Replace that with building work or clearing land (similar output required), and you are less likely to get such a positive response to your invitation. Although the same physical exertion would be needed for either activity, the reaction to the latter may be viewed more negatively, due to being perceived as less fun; one activity is perceived as play and the other as work. The key is to find enjoyment in that activity and gain the most from it, to understand perception is just in our mind.

This distinction between work and play is often instilled into us as children at school. During these formative years, the day is split between lessons and play, with play very much being treated as the reward of work. This is often reinforced at home, with parents insisting children complete homework before playing. If you watch a young child before this has been drummed into them, you will see they are as interested in housework as they are in play, wanting to join in with all activities without prejudice. This is before they have learned which ones they should enjoy and which they should find tedious. This is what we must learn to recapture.

To unlock the key to our full potential, it is essential to engage with every activity fully. Not just with the mind but the heart and body too. This may sound strange to begin with, but by engaging all of yourself, you will find that you become both more efficient and enjoy the task more. This makes the process more rewarding, which in turn is encouraging and will lead to less resistance next time you need to carry out the task.

So, to engage these three areas, we can follow this method: Firstly, it is necessary to engage the body. By sitting up straight, we let ourselves know it is time to focus. Conversely, if you are doing a task that stresses you out, try to adopt a more relaxed position.

Secondly, we need to create an environment that is conducive to work in, which makes it easier to engage our minds. For example, if you are completing paperwork, try to make sure you are undisturbed and working in a quiet room so that you can concentrate.

Thirdly, we engage our hearts (emotions). To do this, you need to know your own heart and what you value in life. Once you understand what you desire, you can use this to motivate yourself to stay on target and to excel.

So, if self-improvement is something you enjoy, aim to develop your skill each time you carry out your task. Wen you are driving your car to work in the morning, see it as practising coordination, reactions, and patience. Need to take a different route? This is a chance to practice memorisation. Perhaps you are having a conversation with someone, but find the subject boring? This can become concentration training. Find the value in each situation.

This can become an enjoyable experience, and tasks that you once dreaded can even start to be the ones you look forward to. You need to find what it is that motivates you and, once you incorporate it in all you do, you will find a noticeable change to how you face challenges in life.

Many people find boredom challenging to deal with. If there are circumstances where there is an unavoidable wait, we can either utilise that time positively or use it as a form of patience training. Within the Zen tradition, mundane work is used as a form of awareness training. In other traditions, such as *Bhakti* yoga, the intention is to perform every task with an act of love. This sense of love for all living creatures is expressed by doing everything to the best standard possible.

When you start to view all challenges with this new outlook, then the world takes on an entirely different colour and light. You will find this beautiful harmonising process starts to become external as well. You begin to harmonise with the world and with everything that is happening.

How to Gain Superhuman Powers

The temple of Apollo in Delphi is famous for an inscription that used to be over the door *Know Thy Self.* I would like to take this opportunity to share with you one of the greatest insights into my own life and, indeed, human nature. An insight I believe, if applied correctly, can lead to great potential in everyday life.

A few years ago, I was musing about the methods we use to influence our subconscious/unconscious mind or self. I started with the contemplation of autosuggestion. Autosuggestion is when you repeat a phrase in the present tense in a commanding tone to influence your subconscious. For example, if you wanted to give up smoking, you would say to yourself, 'I am a non-smoker.' That would get rid of your urges to smoke. Or you could say, 'I am a confident person.' This is an extremely effective method and has been applied for many centuries.

My mind then came to a visualisation which is a method where you imagine what you would like to happen, and you visualise it as clearly and as emotively as you can. You try to make this image sink in as destiny for the future. In that moment, there was a spark of illumination and that these methods are the same methods that our subconscious uses to communicate with us when something is going wrong.

Right now, many people suffer from repetitive thoughts which enter into their mind without them wanting them to, often with a commanding and very present nature. Some people suffer from terrible imaginings that are emotive and very clear. And we go to a doctor or a therapist to try to get rid of these. It dawned on me, there are two selves, and it dawned on me that we are trying to influence each other in the same way when things were going wrong. We only do visualisation and autosuggestion when there is something that has gone off track, and our subconscious does the same when it is trying to influence and tell us about something it is concerned about. In that moment, I realised we have to change our whole attitude about the subconscious or unconscious being negative. We have been viewing something that is a part of us as an element that is to be bludgeoned or forced to do our will. When, in fact, it is our greatest ally. I determined I would look at the effective positive communication that came from my natural mind or my deep mind (as I renamed it). It dawned on me when I received the best information and everything flowed.

First, my deep mind would present an emotion, so it would say to me things are not quite how they seem here, and then when it got my attention, it would explain the details carefully and in order and then would make a gentle suggestion as to what I should do. For example, if I met someone, my deep mind may say to me, 'There is something wrong here, this person is not trustworthy. These things don't add up. You shouldn't do this.' I started to watch for this in everyday life and then started to use the same method back. I wanted a part of myself to change. I wanted my natural self or deep mind to help me. I would start by dwelling on the emotion. And then, when I started moving away from the emotion and it felt right to ask for more information and finally make a request, it worked perfectly with ease.

The breakthrough I experienced was on a day I broke my tooth. I had a terrible toothache, and I could not get an appointment for two weeks. The pain was terrible. I took some time to meditate and dwell on the wish to be free of the pain. When I felt I had gained the right attention, I stated my wish clearly. I knew the tooth was damaged. I promised I would not do anything to hurt it. I would avoid chewing on it and that I would take care of it and that there was an appointment in two weeks. I asked if my natural mind/self could please remove the pain for me, and the pain instantly disappeared.

It did not come back until two weeks past. I foolishly decided that the tooth is not hurting, and I have something more pressing to do, so I will put the appointment off for a day. During that Friday, suddenly the pain came back, I looked at the clock, and it was the time of the appointment. I knew that I had broken the agreement. And that the deep mind, the natural self, in turn, had returned the signal. Since then, I have been practicing this as a skill. It is a skill you need to practice. It is really about making friends with the whole of yourself and integrating as a whole. My experiments are starting to demonstrate through this method you can effortlessly do things that other people would view as superhuman. For example, the ability to memorise large amounts of text at one reading or eliminate hunger when needed. Generate great strength when problems are probably required. I believe this is the next step in our progress that we start to view the whole of ourselves as an ally and working together.

How Harmony Leads to Excellence

Almost all spiritual paths have the goal to achieve a sense of oneness and unity of all things. I believe that to reach our highest potential, we need to move our potential to harmonise with all living things, harmonising with every aspect of life, and harmonising with all the challenges, tasks, and activities that we undertake. By improving our character and transforming ourselves, this philosophy acts like sunlight on the soul. As time goes on, our old sense of self starts to disappear, and we begin to see who we are and discover our true nature.

Many philosophies focus on destroying the ego. I believe the statement. 'I will destroy the ego,' brings the focus back to the confusion. I do not think there is anything to destroy. Instead, I believe a positive, outgoing, caring philosophy where we focus on kindness and living in harmony will bring the results we seek.

The True Hermetic Adept

The true Hermetic adept is both the most invisible and visible of people. His lives out his life in the same way as his fellow man, His outer appearance and actions in life are the same, but with a sense of life and wakefulness few can muster. For him, every breath, thought, and action are holy acts that echoes throughout eternity. For the Hermetic adept, every day is an opportunity to improve oneself even in the smallest way. For him, this is for the greatest joy as he knows that he is one with all of existence and that each small change he makes is a blessing to all living creatures. Due to this, his evolved state of consciousness shines through in every action he makes. When he locks his house, he puts up a protective barrier around it, when he kissed a loved one goodnight, he does so from the heart, and his care for them transfers into a blessing for healing, recovering sleep.

ASSOCIATE WITH THE GOOD IN YOURSELF

CHAPTER 20

Who are you? A question that would take a very long time to answer. We do, however, all have a very complex and specific sense of self. We define ourselves by our words, our actions, and what we wear. It's a very interesting and rewarding exercise to have a look at how you decide when something is part of you. For example, we all know or have met the person who has a terrible habit or addiction but simply does not seem to recognize or accept this fact. In addition to this, I am sure that with your personality there are some aspects of your behaviour that you believe is not the real you, but are something that you have got in the habit of doing. We all have a gold standard, a manner of being that we associate with ourselves aside from external influences. When we are unable to act in accordance with this normal state, we blame our actions and our manner of external influences. 'I'm sorry I was nasty to you, yesterday I was in a bad mood.' But what makes that mood any less part of yourself that the good mood you have today?

The more you penetrate this mystery, the more you tend to realize that very few people are objective about what makes them up. Imagine two people, both with identical habits. In each case, the person spends most of his time being rude and irritable to people and occasionally summons the will to be pleasant and polite. One person may interpret the irritable behaviour and feelings as the real him.

He may say that he is an irritable person and that he tends to have the odd rare burst of optimism that breaks this pattern. Another person might associate with the pleasant side of his personality and say to himself that deep down, he is a happy, pleasant person and that just with the stress of modern living, he finds it hard for him to express the real him. He may even feel that the irritable behaviour is a mask that he wears to protect himself.

Where you draw your line in the sand is a very important and powerful thing. As long as you associate with a type of behaviour or a personality characteristic, it will be tough for you to change, transform, or destroy that aspect of your behaviour. The more you associate with a nature, the more you are that nature. If you have ever worked very hard to change yourself without success, you may find that this is because as much as you want to change, the characteristic is in your mind's past of who you are. This belief is what is holding you back. For success, it is best to have circumspection, honesty and to take a good, look at who you are and how you think and operate. Then you should imagine that all the good characteristics are the real you and that all the negative traits are simply habits that you are withdrawing your force away from all the good in yourself.

RECOGNISING SPIRITUAL TRUTH

CHAPTER 21

When discerning spiritual truth, four principles need to be examined. These are namely feeling, usefulness, knowledge or information, and purpose.

The First Principle of Feeling: Is This Genuine Perception?

Genuine spiritual experience has a specific feel or awareness, which cannot be reproduced by the imagination. For example, let's say you have a strong inclination that someone is going to visit you on a particular day. An excellent way to test if this is a genuine sense or not is to use your imagination then to reproduce the same inkling about something you know not to be true. By imagining the same person doing something that is not true and comparing the two, you can test the first. Genuine spiritual insight will have a sense of clarity and honesty, a specific ring of truth, and a brightness that cannot be reproduced by your imagination.

When doing this, it is important to use the same sense that the insight came in to test it. For example, if you have a strong feeling, test that feeling against a different one in your imagination. If you see a picture in your mind's eye of a specific image or information, imagine a different type of information in your mind's eye and compare the two. You will find when it is a genuine insight, it will appear far brighter, far clearer, and have a specific feel to it. After a few months of practising, you will be able to distinguish the imaginings that are produced by your fears or hopes from those that are from genuine insights.

The Second Principle of Usefulness: Will This Really Work?

Once you have received new information, or a new insight about the nature of how your mind works, or indeed about how the underlying principle of the universe works, then test it.

To do this, imagine yourself as an alchemist in your laboratory. Be detached, do not let self-doubt get in the way of any promising results, but also do not allow the attachment to the joy of this insight get in the way of discarding it if it does not work either. Use this state to apply your new insight to various situations and examine how effective it is. This is when you discover whether your insight, which sounds good, is good.

It is important to do this not just to test if it is true, but also to benefit from genuine insights. This process of testing and applying will make sure that it is embodied and applied, so it becomes a new way of functioning. This is because it's not just important to know how something works but to employ that knowledge practically. To utilise the insight.

The Third Principle of Knowledge and Information: Does it Match Up?

There is a tendency within spiritual communities to lack dedication to empirical investigation of teachings or insights. This is mainly because the information has been received from another source, which is often viewed as beyond scrutiny. However, it is important to apply the same rigours when investigating spiritual truth, as we would if we were applying it to any other knowledge we receive. We should not make an exception just because it has been received from a different source.

Indeed, one should be more careful with such information since we are receiving information from the mind to the mind. With every new insight, compare it with research and the insights of others to verify the information. It is vital to remain emotionally detached, both not to be too close and not to become too critical either.

In the past, I have received specific, valuable information, but after investigation, found that information to be different from historical accounts or that the current research seems to contradict it, and have thus dismissed it. I then doubted the information, but years later found it to be correct. It is important to be very strict with regards to testing our insights, but with practice, we can develop a clear sense of when we should trust our spiritual senses, especially if they work.

The Fourth Principle of Purpose: Why is This Information Being Received?

Sometimes we will find our interests take us down a particular line of investigation. It is essential to ask ourselves firstly, for what reason are we receiving this information, and secondly, for what purpose are we researching this subject? If, after this, you find that what you are getting from it is some form of emotional stimulation, such as approval from others, then it is time to question the motives behind this course of action. Moreover, if the primary purpose does not aid you with your evolution or helping others, it may not be as genuine as you might think, and you need to investigate further.

Now with these principles, if you have learned to apply them correctly, you will be able to naturally look to the stars while keeping your feet firmly on the ground. These principles can also be applied to other sources of spiritual information, for example, a book. Let us use this to examine how all four principles can be applied.

To begin with, we use our senses or intuition to feel if the book is right. You have probably noticed when you read certain books, somehow, they feel alive. For me, the sense of how it makes me feel often reflects the wisdom of the book and, when reading such information that is genuine and speaks of truth, you will find it is also significant to your life. The resonance of such words tends to have a balancing effect on your emotional state, and it is this kind of literature that we are looking to gain nourishment from. It is possible to test these techniques to see if they work. You can do this by comparing the information you receive with other authorities and other people's experiences. It is good to observe and explore the reasons why you are investigating this particular subject. Often the 'why' may just be exploring, but it is important to have clarity in your reasoning. Otherwise, it could be the case where time-consuming studies are undertaken which may not be of any benefit to you.

These four principles can also be applied to people. For example, when listening to a spiritual teacher, be aware of the feel of what they are saying. This can be compared to falsehood in your imagination. You can test them directly with a lie. You could ask them a question such as, 'I sensed guru that you healed me last night, is that true?' If they reply, 'Yes, I did that,' then maybe their discernment is not to be trusted.

It is also possible to test out and observe their level of ability and technique to see if they are capable of doing what they say they can do. It is a useful practice to do since it is an indication of what skills you will be able to obtain from that particular teacher.

Are Their Students Getting the Same Results?

It has often been said that we now live in the Age of Information, and it is easy to see why. So much knowledge is accessible in the world due to the internet, and with fewer hurdles to publishing ideas, we have so many more 'experts' offering their services too. Unfortunately, in many cases, the evidence points to the contrary, and they have yet to achieve the very results they are advertising you can gain by following them. One example of this is the trendy schemes that purport to make money without much work. In fact, under scrutiny, most people in the system are not making money, and those at the top who may be, are usually more reliant on those desperate people signing up at the bottom than whatever they claim is making them the money. This same model, with a lack of expertise at the top supported by the emotions of those below, is evident within many spiritual communities.

Many people claim to have vast knowledge or amazing past lives where they were very competent and extraordinary people, but do not show any qualities being associated with either being able to apply that knowledge or possessing any of these abilities from that past life to the now. Of course, you can test what they say against other people's research and of trusted texts within that tradition, but if they are unable to apply it to their own life, then how are they going to help you to apply it to yours?

It is also important to question why certain information has been given to you. If this information does not have a direct relationship in assisting you in some way, ask yourself these three questions:

1. Why has this information been given to me?
2. For what purpose am I being told this information?
3. Who does this information benefit?

It is important to question the motives of these actions. Often there are fascinating insights and very important things that are told to students; however, it becomes a part of an exciting play, where everyone feels a lot better since it enhances their status. It is essential to look at the why, and if the why is strongly motivated by a financial motive, then maybe the validity of information should be brought into question.

By applying these principles on all levels, we gain the ability to be completely genuine. This is important because it is necessary to have spiritual clarity, honour, and truth above all things.

FURTHER METHODS TO STILL OR FOCUS THE MIND

CHAPTER 22

If you ever find it hard to make progress no matter what you do in your practice sessions, and you find that your skill or ability is not improving, one of the most important things I can advise is to take that skill and apply it in your normal life. For example, if you are learning to concentrate, really use that concentration. If you are learning to watch your thoughts, learn to observe not just your thoughts, but those of others and the underlying pattern around you. For those wanting to develop inner silence, learn to be silent or restrained in actions and situations that call for it in daily life. If you are tuning into the great good these methods should be seen as a doorway to that oneness.

These principles can be applied to all exercises, including those of visualisation or involving energy once you apply these exercises with their intended cause. When you return to your original exercise, you will notice a difference. It is essential to realise the exercise is not the goal. It is what it says. It is just an exercise to give you a new level of ability to be used in other circumstances as well.

Here is a list of practical methods to aid in meditation progress.

Watch and Focus

This method is the most common form of meditation. An object is chosen to concentrate the mind on. This point of focus can be of any sense. It can be real or imaginary. It could be the image of a deity or the sound of a bell. It could even be the sensation of air coming in and out of your nose. Many traditions use mandalas or pictures for this practice. As long as the stimulus is not too changeable, the mind will continue to be calm and relaxed. When it does, the meditator will only be moved by his deep emotional mind. By watching his disturbances, the meditator can learn about himself.

Focus on a Point

This method involves focusing on one point on your body. Unlike the previous method, nothing is imagined, and no sensation is focused on. You just simply keep your awareness on the chosen point. The two most common points to focus on are your third eye or your centre of gravity (*dantian*), a location on your belly three-finger distances below your navel. Whenever the meditator's mind drifts, it is brought back to that point of focus. Eventually, the mind will be slow and calm. Then again, your distractions will only be ones caused by your emotional mind.

Watch Your Breath

This method is the safest and easiest for the beginner. I recommend this method to be used by anyone regardless of their level of development. In this method, the meditator simply watches his or her breathing pattern. Pay attention to the rhythm of the breath and the sensations. This is not to say that the focus shifts but to mention that this stimulus is felt during the process. As the meditation goes on, the meditator may become aware of the sound of his breath. Whenever your mind drifts, just bring it back to your breathing. Soon your mind will become quiet. It is worth noting that this meditation is often combined with one of the above methods. For example, the sensation of the breath can be the focus or light visualized as the breath. Sometimes the practitioner breathes into a certain point in the body. Each tradition has its tricks and methods. What matters is persistence.

Holding Back the Tide

This is the hardest method of meditation. The meditator simply stops their thoughts, to hold back thoughts, and resist any thoughts appearing. This method is known to cause mental problems to come to the forefront and can develop the mind in an unbalanced way. For this reason, this method is not recommended for those who are not following a complete and balanced spiritual path. Repeating sacred texts or a phrase is another very effective method. Typically, when using a phrase or a mantra, it would be repeated either out loud or in your mind's eye with each out-breath. This way, your mind has to concentrate on the action as well as the sound. Likewise, performing a dance can be a very good form of this meditation. This repeated method is straightforward and effective. It is so effective that sometimes not even the emotional mind can distract us. Thus, it is perfect for relaxation but not for learning about yourself or overcoming mental problems.

OTHER FORMS OF HERMETIC MEDITATION

CHAPTER 23

Hermetic Practice of Inner Silence

Within the Western tradition, there are records with descriptions of a meditative practice of inner silence. This Hesychia, an ancient Greek term meaning inner silence, had very different associations and a specific feel to it, which is not comparable to the practice laid out in most oriental traditions. Silence is seen as a holy thing, a form of prayer because no words can truly express the scheme of totality. When you sit in silence, this is a raising of your awareness, bringing forth your full potential and taking on a divine quality.

Silence, goodness, and awareness are one and the same quality. When you silence your mind, you are taking aspects of yourself that normally are out of harmony or out of your control and uniting them into one state of consciousness as a raising of the self. This is the practice of silence within the Western tradition, whereby we bring our full potential without any inner noise. We can see things how they really are and observe things beyond; thus, through this practice, we can connect with our true divine nature.

The Hermetic Equivalent of the OM (ॐ)

Many people will know of the Hindu mantra OM. OM is a sacred word within the yogic tradition said to be the word that underlies the whole of existence and even the sound that created the whole of existence. It is used as a mantra, if not the ultimate mantra, whereby the yogic practitioner will repeat OM with regularity and unmoving steady focus to raise their consciousness to new heights. Many people have contemplated whether or not there is an equivalent in the Hermetic or Western tradition.

CHAPTER 23 OTHER FORMS OF HERMETIC MEDITATION

The most common comparison is to do with the vision of Hermes and the story of creation in Hermeticism. When Hermes experienced his vision, he went into a deep state of meditation. Right at the beginning, he sees a beautiful divine light start to condense into more dense levels of existence. At that point, he hears an intelligible word like a moan come forth, and many people have wondered if that moan sounded like the OM sound. Hermes not being educated in the Indian tradition saw this as a noise rather than a word. Other people have compared OM to a slightly different area of Hermetic creation, whereby the word, logos, enters existence, giving the underlying structure and laws to everything.

If we read the ancient papyri [5] of the Western tradition, we see many different powerful phrases used. Some of them are used as a firm statement of intent, or to bring about a particular influence, but others are used for repetition. What stands out as the most powerful and respected is the singing of the seven vowels. The seven Greek vowels were connected with seven notes and seven planets. We know from accounts by the practitioners of the Egyptian tradition it was beautiful and sounded like a beautiful instrument or the sound from a higher or purer place.

If you read the initiation or self-initiation rites, they often use this phrase of seven vowels, and some authorities assert that a different musical note was put at each of the different vowels. If this is true, the practitioners in those days were far more musically skilled than most of us are nowadays. Trying to sync each different letter on a different note is so cumbersome a technique, it gets in the way of the state of mind, at least from my own observational experience. This phrase was used to raise the consciousness to the great good. It was a phrase that would help you step up the different planetary spheres inside yourself and maybe even externally so you could visit these spheres and different places. Other texts say this is the spell or hymn sung at your birth as your soul goes down through the planetary spheres as it takes on the qualities and personality that you will have, and you can, in turn, use it to lift yourself back up.

So how would you use this formula as a means for Hermetic meditation to tune into the great good? I believe this was handled very differently than we would see mantras. I believe often it was in a group and was undoubtedly ecstatic. Rather than a repetition that helps change the consciousness by its regularity and focus, this was used ecstatically. You are going to increase your awareness, increase your emotional dedication, and lift your consciousness into a higher sphere with every repetition. You can imagine how powerful in a group setting this would be. And with each repetition, stepping higher and higher, you would move towards climax a culmination, a spiritual vision, at the end. The feel of it is more shamanic than yogic in expression. The vowels demonstrated by me. [6]

---

[5] See Greek vowels and the Chaldean planets: http://voces-magicae.com/2009/12/17/greek-vowels-and-the-chaldean-planets/

[6] See Greek vowels and the Chaldean planets: http://voces-magicae.com/2009/12/17/greek-vowels-and-the-chaldean-planets/ https://www.youtube.com/watch?v=DCasDYTkekc

ABOUT THE AUTHOR

Martin Faulks has dedicated his life to the mastery of life through the mastery of the art of meditation. His mission has always been to seek out the human potential that lies within all of us and to harness for the betterment of oneself and others to quote:

My Inner quest is to discover my full potential through the art of meditation, to use this skill to make the most of my time on earth and have the most beneficial effect while I am here. To bring out the best in myself in order to be of best service to the world......

Through diligent unbroken disciplined practice, he has gained the fruits of such endeavours' which he shares with us all today. He has over twenty years' experience as a practitioner in this art including extensive studies that have involved travelling around the world in search to further his knowledge on the subject. He generously shares with us the keys to success in meditation, which are also transposable into our everyday lives.

For me, meditation is the ultimate skill, the mastery of which leads to mastery of all other skills.

~ Martin Faulks

One of his greatest achievements is that of personal development and overcoming obstacles and challenges in his own life through applying the same principles that apply in meditation.

Only when our knowledge of inner Technologies and abilities matches our outer Progress will we reach our full potential.

His achievements are testimony to this. They include running the Seshen Meditation School, which is dedicated to the growth and self-mastery of its students. His studies have allowed him to be successful in all areas of life, including the world of business. He is an accomplished martial artist who began at the age of five years old. He has also demonstrated the power of meditation in controlling the elemental forces such as sub-zero temperatures as well as superhuman strength.

Not only has he dedicated his life to self-mastery but also assisted countless others in their path to self-development through his extensive knowledge of the subject. Lastly, his positivity and humility leave a lasting impression on you.

The potential that lies in our own Consciousness, if used correctly, never ceases to amaze me, and I believe that it is through this inner study we as a race can learn to live in greater harmony with our own bodies and with the world around us. Of course, the greatest lessons come from practice and, through diligent daily dedication to the art of meditation for over 20 years, I have gained what I believe is a clear vision of the full potential in us all. How the vibrations created through our meditation can become one with our daily consciousness.

Martin Faulks

www.martinfaulks.com

www.ingramcontent.com/pod-product-compliance
Lightning Source LLC
Chambersburg PA
CBHW040930240426
43672CB00021B/2993